KARA ZUARO

I LIKE FOOD

FOOD TASTES GOOD

In the Kitchen with Your Favorite Bands

HYPERION NEW YORK

KARA ZUARO

I LIKE FOOD

FOOD TASTES GOOD

In the Kitchen with Your Favorite Bands

HYPERION NEW YORK

Library of Congress Cataloging-in-Publication Data
Zuaro, Kara.
  I like food, food tastes good : in the kitchen with your favorite bands / by Kara Zuaro.
    p. cm.
   ISBN: 1-4013-0874-0
   ISBN-13: 978-14013-0874-2
  1. Cookery. 2. Rock groups. I. Title.
 TX714 .Z83 2007
 641.5 22   2006049692

Hyperion books are available for special promotions and premiums. For details contact Michael Rentas, Assistant Director, Inventory Operations, Hyperion, 77 West 66th Street, 12th floor, New York, New York 10023-6298, or call 212-456-0133.

Design by Fritz Metsch

FIRST EDITION

10 9 8 7 6 5 4 3 2 1

FOR PETE

–KZ

CONTENTS

CHAPTER ONE: BREAKFAST

Bling Kong	BIG APPLE QUICHE PUFFS	4
Calexico	TOFU SCRAMBLE	6
Dr. Dog	MOM'S MUFFIN BREAD	7
Maserati	SOUTHERN CHEESE GRITS	9
Roots of Orchis	SWEET POTATO BISCUITS AND VEGAN VEGETABLE GRAVY	*11*
Silkworm	CHEESY SLEAZY	*15*
Smoosh	*VARLDENS BASTA PANNKAKA*	*17*

CHAPTER TWO: SOUPS, SIDES, AND STARTERS

Battles	ROASTED BONE MARROW "BATTLES STYLE"	*21*
Birds of Avalon	NOT-SO-GREASY GREENS	24
The Black Hollies	"HAVE MERCY ON ME" LENTIL SOUP	27
Brakes	HEALTHY GREEN SOUP	30
Craig Wedren	BAKED BRIE	32
The Descendents	BILL'S *PICO DE GALLO*	34
Edie Sedgwick	BRUSSELS SPROUTS À LA DENZEL WASHINGTON	35
Enon	A RECIPE FOR THE ONE WHO IS GETTING SOME KIND OF COLD	38
Headlights	ROCK 'N' ROLL RANGOON	40
Komakino	GARLIC MUSHY PEAS	42
Mojave 3	LEEK & POTATO SOUP	44
Pegasuses-XL	THE SECRET TOBIAS FAMILY POTATO PANCAKE RECIPE	46

The Rosebuds	ZUCCHINI SLIPPERS	48
Scoville Unit	THE SCOVILLE TORTILLA	50
Sorry About Dresden	LIFE OF THE PARTY CHICKEN ON A STICK	53
Viva Voce	BEST GUACAMOLE EVER & HOTT BOILED PEANUTS	55

CHAPTER THREE: SANDWICHES

Amphetameanies	HAM-FETA-BEANIE	61
Belle & Sebastian	HRT—HALLOUMI, RADICCHIO, AND TOMATO SANDWICH	62
Chris Mills	BOLOGNA, MUSTARD, AND PICKLE SANDWICH	63
Death Cab for Cutie	VEGGIE SAUSAGE AND PEANUT BUTTER SANDWICH	64
Hayden	EXPLODING SANDWICH	65
Hudson Bell	RIVERBOATS	67
Mates of State	PEAR AND GOAT CHEESE *PANINI*	68
M. Ward	KERI'S VEGAN GREEK SANDWICHES	69
My Morning Jacket	THE "YOU CAN CARE IF YOU WANNA" SANDWICH	71

CHAPTER FOUR: MAIN COURSES FOR CARNIVORES

THE MEAT SECTION

Aluminum Group	PASTA BOLOGNESE	75
The Decemberists	PORK LOIN WITH POBLANO CHILIES	77
Grandaddy	BBQ STEAK	79
The Hold Steady	MIDWESTERN-STYLE BRATWURST	81
The Long Winters	ALASKA-STYLE MACARONI SOUP *AL CARNE*	84
NOFX	EL HEFE'S SPECIALTIES	89
Rahim	SAUERBRATEN	91
Rye Coalition	PORK CHOPS SALVEMINI	93
The Violent Femmes	WILD BOAR *RAGÙ*	95

THE POULTRY SECTION

Aloha — FRIED CHICKEN WITH BISCUITS AND GRAVY — 97

Dälek — SPICY *ARROZ CON POLLO* — 99

Drew Isleib — CHICKEN IN COCONUT CURRY — 101

Racebannon — BRANDY PEACH SAUCE FOR CHICKEN OR TOFU — 103

Slowdive — CHICKEN FILO PESTO PARCEL WITH PUY PUY — 105

Strung Out — ROCK 'N' RAMEN — 108

tommygun — SWEET POTATO–MANGO–CHICKEN QUESADILLAS — 110

The Walkmen — FOREIGN CHICKEN DINNER — 112

Windsor for the Derby — SPICY WINGS À LA CHICKIE — 115

THE FISH SECTION

Centro-matic — SOUTH SAN GABRIEL SWEET POTATOES AND SALMON — 117

Crooked Fingers — SEARED TUNA WITH WASABI-COCONUT SAUCE AND ROASTED-PEPPER RICE PILAF — 119

Kings of Convenience — WOLF FISH À *L'ITALIA* — 122

Mobius Band — TROPICAL FISH TACOS — 124

Patrick Phelan — SWANKY MAC AND CHEESE — 126

RJD2 — FISH TACOS WITH AVOCADOS — 129

S.A. Smash — ROOFTOP PARTY SALMON — 131

The Velvet Teen — SPAGHETTI WITH CLAM CHOWDER SAUCE — 132

CHAPTER 5: MAIN COURSES FOR VEGETARIANS

The Bad Plus — *ORECCHIETTE* WITH BROCCOLI RABE — 136

Camera Obscura — VEGETARIAN PAELLA — 138

The Concretes — TOMATO SAUCE FOR PASTA — 140

Heston Rifle — BAKED BARBECUE TOFU — 142

Houston McCoy — EGGPLANT PARMESAN — 144

Imperial Teen — EDDIE VEDDER STEW — 147

Kudzu Wish — CURRY VARIATIONS — 148

Little Wings — UNCLE KYLE'S AVOCADO TACOS — 151

Lucero	SPINACH LASAGNA	152
Maplewood	NIGHT-BEFORE-TOUR MAC AND CHEESE	154
Matt Pond PA	VEGETABLE ENCHILADAS WITH HOMEMADE TOMATILLO SALSA	157
The Mountain Goats	TATO MATO	160
Murder by Death	SPICED TOFU STIR-FRY	163
Now It's Overhead	QUICK CHICKPEAS	165
Rapider Than Horsepower	TOFU POTPIE	167
The Reputation	ASIAN STIR-FRY FOR VEGETARIANS WHO HATE VEGETABLES	169
Shearwater	THOR'S BLACK BEAN NACHOS	171
Superchunk	"THAI" GRILLED MARINATED TOFU	173
Ted Leo and the Pharmacists	SEMI-RAW EVERYDAY PASTA	175
Voxtrot	PEANUTTY BLACK-BEAN TOFU	178

CHAPTER 6: DRINKS

Bratmobile	PARTY AT YOUR OWN RISK SANGRIA	183
Early Day Miners	THE KARATE KID	184
The Forms	CAMILOFLAGE	185
Irving	DIRTY SNOWFLAKE	187
Laura Minor	DARK 'N' STORMY FLORIDA & FLORIDA EAST COAST CHAMPION SWEET TEA	188
Nada Surf	PATRIOT ACT *MOJITOS*	191
Swearing at Motorists	THE JOHN GLENN	192
They Might Be Giants	COUNTRYPOLITAN	193
Vague Angels	VEGAN SKY JUICE	194

CHAPTER 7: DESSERTS

Ben Kweller	CHOCOLATE BALLS	199
Catfish Haven	STRAWBERRY POP CAKE	201

Devendra Banhart	AFRICANITAS RICAS	203
Drive-By Truckers	SISSY'S BANANA PUDDING	205
Franz Ferdinand	LEMON GINGER FLAPJACKS	209
Frog Eyes	CHOCOLATE WORM	211
Grizzly Bear	PECAN PIE	213
Interpol	*CACAO ROSSO*	214
John Vanderslice	ONE-DISH FRESH-FRUIT COBBLER	216
Les Savy Fav	BUTTERSCOTCH PIE	218
Northern State	7-LAYER BARS	219
Okkervil River	BUTTERMILK PIE	221
Pelican	OATMEAL CAKE	224
Portastatic	CHOCOLATE CHIP PIE	226
Ris Paul Ric	VEGAN CHOCOLATE CHIP COOKIES	228
Shonen Knife	HEALTHY GREEN COOKIES	230
Tilly and the Wall	"BACON AND EGGS"	232
Umphrey's McGee	KAHLÚA CAKE	234
Index		237

ACKNOWLEDGMENTS

This book was born over a meal with my friend Brian Bedsworth, who has since served as its co-editor. I can't thank him enough for planting the seed for this project. I'd also like to thank those who helped it grow into a real book; Shannon O'Keefe (my literary agent, my dear friend, and my favorite cohort for preparing multicourse meals), Emily Gould and Zareen Jaffery (my editors), and Jason Munn of Small Stakes (the artist responsible for the book's pitch-perfect cover). Also, big hugs and thanks to my parents, for raising me on rock 'n' roll and giving me rein of their kitchen. And, thanks, of course, to all the bands who shared recipes; I am making a donation to Share Our Strength, an antihunger charity, in their honor.

Also, thanks to all the great people who helped me track down these recipes, especially Caroline Borolla at AAM, Vanessa Burt at Fat Wreck Chords, Ezra Careaff at Slowdance, Mike Conklin at the *L Magazine*, Pete D'Angelo and Gandhar Savur at Ernest Jenning, Lyle Hysen at Bank Robber, Wes Howerton at Barsuk, Dana Meyerson at Biz 3, Pam Nashel Leto at Girlie Action, Carla Parisi at Tijuana Gift Shop, Jonny Richardson at Secretly Canadian, Traci Thomas at New West, Julie Underwood at Tag Team, Phil Waldorf and Dylan Siegler, and my sister, Kyle Zuaro.

INTRODUCTION

Many of the contributors to this cookbook have not had a home-cooked meal in weeks. For the most part, they've eschewed stable careers (and stable incomes) to see the world through the window of a van. Someday they may have to face the inside of a cubicle, but for now, they're heading to Charlotte, then Raleigh, then Richmond. For the foreseeable future, they'll party professionally and bring joy and hangovers to every city they visit. Their weekends never end. They're a wandering community of big drinkers and independent thinkers. They're doing what they love. They're happy. They're broke. And they're hungry.

The hungry part didn't occur to me until I met Aloha at a South Bend, Indiana, coffee shop, back in college. I was writing my very first show review about their performance, and I really had no idea how to go about doing it, so I tried to engrave their loose-limbed, jazz-based set into my memory. I can still see how they positioned themselves in an inward-facing circle in the center of the room, and how the coffee drinkers rose, one by one, to surround them. A very small boy, about five or six years old, squeezed up past the mic stand and stood at the singer's feet, gazing upward. The vibraphone player pounded out melodies that swam circles around the others in the smoky air, and I was standing so close to the amp that I could feel the bass-line throbbing inside my rib cage, like a second heartbeat.

After the show, when I politely asked the bass player, Matthew Gengler, if they were having a nice time on tour, he spoke very matter-of-factly into my brand-new mini-tape recorder: "I'm tired and I'm hungry. I can't wait to go home." Aloha hadn't eaten dinner that night. They couldn't remember if they'd eaten anything since they'd had Taco Bell the night before. I wished I had some sandwiches to pass out, but I didn't even have enough money in my pocket to buy them a round of coffees.

After college, I moved to Brooklyn and I always cooked for my friends' bands when they passed through town. Over one of those tour dinners, my friend Brian Bedsworth (formerly of Disband) and I decided to start compiling recipes from all our musician friends—we figured we could put together some handmade cookbooks to give as Christmas gifts or maybe even sell at shows. During interviews with bands, I started asking about their favorite foods, and Brian hit up every band in North Carolina for recipes. We quickly learned that conversations about food shed a whole new light on our favorite bands. While they might not *all* have the most refined palates, they do tend to appreciate eating—a daily activity that most of us take for granted. In some small way, each recipe here is a testament to life's simple pleasures (even the one that involves a boil-in-bag steak and optional green food coloring). So take a bite. Smile. Repeat.

I LIKE FOOD

FOOD TASTES GOOD

BREAKFAST | **ONE**

LET'S BE HONEST HERE—the only touring band that is up early enough to sip coffee and savor crisp slices of bacon as the sun rises is a band that hasn't gone to bed yet. Greasy food—especially when consumed after the club closes and before the sleeping bags are unrolled—does wonders to soak up a hangover, but unless a band is crashing with a dutiful cook who is also their best friend, the chances of getting a hot meal at four thirty in the morning are slim. If you happen to be one of these rare, wonderful, and sleep-deprived hosts or hostesses, this chapter is dedicated to you. But before you break out one of these recipes—whether it's the wee hours of the morning or just feels like it—there is one key question that you must ask yourself first: "How drunk am I?"

If you're really wasted, then chances are you're not the only one. You should save yourself some trouble and just whip up some scrambled eggs for your drunken guests. If there's a vegan in the house, make Calexico's Tofu Scramble, but for goodness' sake, please be careful chopping up all those vegetables. Perhaps you should let the vegan do it. Smoosh's giant pancake is easy to make, too, but if you pass out during the forty-five minutes it takes to bake, it'll burn to a crisp, set off your fire alarm, and wake up your roommates. (If your roommates' names are Mom and Dad, this will be especially unfortunate.) Better yet, you can make breakfast ahead of time—Dr. Dog's muffin bread keeps well in the fridge and can be popped into the toaster whenever the band comes home.

However, if your buzz is wearing off, or you just woke up still moderately drunk from last night, you're going to want to put in a little extra effort for a dish that will soothe your impending headache and nausea. Silkworm's fool-proof Cheesy Sleazy works like magic, and Bling Kong's Big Apple Quiche Puffs are another safe bet—just be sure to make extra bacon so your guests can snack on it while the puffs are in the oven. Maserati's Southern Cheese Grits are great, too, as long as you can focus on stirring them constantly so they don't get too thick or stick to the pan.

Only if you're stone-cold sober should you endeavor to prepare the Sweet Potato

Biscuits and Vegan Vegetable Gravy from Roots of Orchis. These are fine recipes, but they're time-consuming and require your undivided attention. Someone who is seeing double should not be browning flour.

Once you decide which recipe best corresponds with your state of inebriation, cook it up like the hero that you are, pair it with aspirin, coffee, and copious amounts of water, revel in compliments to the chef, and then direct your best friend's band to the couch so you can finally get some rest.

from Liz "Shredder" Schroeter

BIG APPLE QUICHE PUFFS

With four cheerleaders, three drummers, two guitarists, a bass player, a veejay, and some-times a horn section, New York's Bling Kong doesn't put on a show so much as a down-and-dirty spectacle. The band's lyrics are way too racy to recount here, especially because Liz "Shredder" Schroeter comes from a long line of church-going domestic goddesses who will probably read this page. (Hi, Grandma Helen!) When you're food shopping for this one, don't cheap out and get the store-brand biscuits, unless you're sure they're as big as Pillsbury Crescent Rolls Big N Flaky. If they're too small, they won't wrap around the fill-ing properly and your puffs won't look as professional.

"For years my grandma, a two-time Pillsbury Bake-Off finalist and winner of many regional chicken, beef, and other cooking-champ awards, has been urging me to enter the Pillsbury Bake-Off. 'You can win a million dollars!' she tells me. Now I'm hardly the cook that my grandma, or even my mother, is (Mom cans her own pickles and jams—hot items at church fund-raisers!), but I do love food and cash prizes, so I gave it a shot. Since moving to NYC, I have found a certain comfort in a delicious breakfast sandwich on a rough morning, especially after a particularly intoxicating Bling Kong show, and that's what inspired the Big Apple Quiche Puffs. I incorporated the requisite Pillsbury item and invented these warm, puffy, gooey, and delicious bacon, apple, and cheese quiche puffs."

—LIZ "SHREDDER" SCHROETER

INGREDIENTS:

Nonstick cooking spray

1 can Pillsbury Crescent Rolls Big N Flaky

1 large, tart baking apple, thinly sliced

6 slices cooked bacon, broken into small
    pieces

1 1/2 cups grated cheddar cheese

6 eggs

3 tablespoons milk

1/2 teaspoon salt

GARNISH IF DESIRED:

Fresh basil, finely chopped, or green onion

1. Preheat oven to 350°F. Spray a 9" x 13" baking pan. Separate the crescents and arrange them so that half of each crescent is in the pan, and the other half is hanging out over the edge. (After you add the other ingredients, you'll be folding the crescents over the top of your breakfast creation.)

2. Arrange 3–4 apple slices on top of each crescent (the part that's in the pan, of course), and layer with bacon and cheese.

3. In a bowl, beat eggs, milk, and salt. Pour over the contents of pan, and then fold crescent corners over the apples, cheese, bacon, and egg mixture. (The crescents won't cover the dish completely, but they do make a nice pattern over eggs.)

4. Bake at 350°F for 20 minutes, or until rolls are golden brown and eggs are set.

5. Let cool for 5 minutes before cutting into pieces to serve.

Makes 6 servings.

from Joey Burns

TOFU SCRAMBLE

Core members Joey Burns (vocals, guitar) and John Convertino (drums, percussion) are Calexico's only constant. Zigzagging across the borders of indie rock, Latin music, country, blues, and jazz, the Tucson-based band has been known to collaborate with a boisterous mariachi band on one record and join forces with Iron & Wine, purveyors of hushed and delicate folk, on the next. Like Calexico's ever-changeable sound, Joey's Tofu Scramble can be enjoyed in a number of ways. Serve as an alternative to scrambled eggs for breakfast or stuff it into some tortillas for a simple dinner. To give this dish a kick, pick up a can of chipotle peppers in *adobo* sauce and add a super-spicy minced chile to your skillet with the onion and tofu—or just hit it with your favorite hot sauce.

INGREDIENTS:

Half a yellow onion, diced

1 package of extra-firm tofu, cubed

Olive oil

1 yellow squash, diced

1 zucchini, diced

Half a red bell pepper, diced

4 cloves of garlic, sliced

Bunch of fresh spinach, coarsely chopped

DIRECTIONS:

1. Sauté diced yellow onion along with cubed tofu and olive oil in cast-iron skillet until gently browned.
2. Add diced yellow squash and zucchini.
3. After a short while add diced red bell pepper.
4. Lastly, add sliced garlic cloves and fresh spinach.
5. After the spinach wilts, remove from heat.
6. Serve on its own or with tortillas.

Serves 2–3.

from Zach's mom, Kathy Miller

MOM'S MUFFIN BREAD

Dr. Dog, a good-times five-piece from the suburbs of Philly, travels with an arsenal of catchy tunes. Their most irresistible sing-along, "Wake Up," may be the best breakfast anthem of all time, but recipe contributor and keyboardist Zach Miller doesn't come from a family of breakfast lovers. "I know a lot of people (myself included) who relish the opportunity to make a large, elaborate breakfast, but we never did that growing up," he laments. "It was either eggs/toast/coffee or waffles, never potatoes or fruit or omelets. My dad usually only has a glass of chocolate milk for breakfast, but he loves to add a piece of muffin bread when it's available." This simple, cornmeal-crusted loaf hits the spot and stays fresh for days. Flavor-wise, it has more in common with an English muffin than muffins of the bran or banana-nut varieties.

"This is my mom's muffin bread, which was a staple in our house growing up. Now I make it on my own and it's one of my favorite things in the world. I like mine toasted with butter, which is so good I've never risked trying it any other way. Serve next to some coffee or chocolate milk." —ZACH MILLER

INGREDIENTS:

2 packages active dry yeast

1/2 cup warm water

5–6 cups flour

2 tablespoons sugar

1/2 teaspoon baking soda

2 teaspoons salt

2 cups milk, warmed

1/4 cup butter

cornmeal for pans

EQUIPMENT:

Two 81/2" x 41/2" pans

1. Preheat oven to 400°F. Grease two 8 1/2" x 4 1/2" loaf pans and sprinkle them with cornmeal. Set aside.

2. In a mixing bowl, dissolve yeast in warm water.

3. Stir in 2 cups flour, the sugar, and the baking soda.

4. Now add the salt and then one more cup of flour.

5. In a pan, heat the milk and butter until warm (it should feel hot, but not scalding, when you stick your finger in it) and add to mixture. Beat well.

6. Stir in remaining flour to make a stiff batter. Divide and pour into the two prepared loaf pans.

7. Sprinkle the tops with a little cornmeal. Cover with a towel, some foil, or some plastic wrap, and let rise 45 minutes in a warm place.

8. When the dough has risen near the tops of the pans, pop them into the oven and bake for 25 minutes until hollow-sounding when tapped. Remove from pans immediately and cool.

9. Slice, toast, butter, and enjoy. I store one loaf in the fridge while in use and the other in the freezer.

And here's one more serving suggestion: One of my favorite meals of all time is to toast and butter up the muffin bread and top it off with spoonfuls of Cream of Wheat with honey. Gross to most, but trust me, it's really, really good. I don't know why it slipped my mind before, but there it is.

Makes 2 loaves.

from Matt Cherry

SOUTHERN CHEESE GRITS

A slightly skeevy biker bar on Long Island is an unlikely place to find a fledgling instrumental rock band from Athens, Georgia, but that's where I met Maserati back in the summer of 2001. Matt Cherry, their friendly guitarist, cheerfully described his band's sound to me as "Gritty yet melodic!" and gave me a free CD and his phone number so we could hang out in the city before they left town. Several tours and countless cell-phone minutes later, we're as close as two friends could possibly be—without ever living in the same state.

The first time Maserati crashed at my Brooklyn apartment, I wanted to offer them a big morning meal before they got back in the van, but I felt kind of stupid asking a bunch of hungover dudes if they wanted brunch. For some reason, "brunch" never sounds very punk rock. Anyway, I mentioned as casually as possible that I'd thrown together a hash-brown casserole the day before and had some eggs in the fridge. The next thing I knew, Matt was handing me cutting boards full of perfectly diced onions, deftly flipping omelets, scrubbing the dishes, wiping down the counters, and crawling around my kitchen floor with a dustpan. It's nice to have friends who get as fired-up about brunch as I do.

At Matt's house, a big breakfast often includes a plate of his stick-to-your ribs cheese grits. This probably goes without saying for Southern cooks, but for all you Yankees out there, you'll find grits in the oatmeal aisle, and you should get the old-fashioned (not instant) kind.

"If you've lived or spent significant amounts of time in the South, you know that grits are a staple of the Southern breakfast palette. Grits are basically a type of corn porridge and don't really have much of a taste by themselves, so you've got to focus on the consistency. The grits served at Waffle House, for example, tend to be thin and watery, but this recipe makes thick and creamy grits. Recently, grits seemed to have caught on in gourmet restaurants all over the place. I went to a restaurant in Ann Arbor, Michigan, where they serve a plate of cheese grits for about eight dollars. The funny thing is that you can get a twenty-pound sack of grits in the South for that price." —MATT CHERRY

3 cups water

1 cup grits

1/2 cup milk

4 tablespoons butter

1–2 teaspoons salt, or to taste

2 teaspoons black pepper

4 ounces sharp white cheddar cheese, cut
  into small pieces

DIRECTIONS:

1. Heat the water in a small saucepan until it comes to a boil.
2. Turn the heat down to a low simmer, add the grits, stir, and cover. Stir occasionally, ensuring that the grits do not stick to the bottom of the pan.
3. After about 10–12 minutes, the grits will have soaked up all the water (the mixture should be thick, not watery). Add the milk and stir thoroughly.
4. Add the butter, salt, pepper, and cheese. Stir constantly for a minute or two, until the cheese is melted and the mixture has a creamy consistency.

This makes a great side dish to a breakfast of eggs, bacon, or sausage, and toast. It can also be used as a bed for blackened chicken, fish, or shrimp.

Serves 4.

from Jackie Musick

SWEET POTATO BISCUITS AND VEGAN VEGETABLE GRAVY

I was ordering breakfast tacos at my favorite Austin eatery, Maria's Taco Xpress, when my friend Dylan spotted some familiar faces at the salsa and *chimichurri* bar. Apparently, Roots of Orchis were friends with her boss at the architecture firm where she interned and she recognized them from the time she saw them sleeping on the office floor. We sat at adjacent tables on the restaurant's ramshackle patio and discussed Jackie's surprisingly sophisticated vegan gravy, which really has no business being as good as it is. The first time I made it, my roommate, Timmy, and my boyfriend, Pete, chatted about the glory of Cracker Barrel's real (that is, non-vegan) biscuits and gravy. They watched skeptically as I rolled sticky orange dough with the side of a beer bottle and then began to sauté some dry flour. It took a while to put everything together, but when I was finally done, the boys were scarfing the biscuits and licking the gravy bowl. Don't expect this to taste like traditional biscuits and gravy—but it is a very tasty food unto itself.

SWEET POTATO BISCUITS

"This is a great recipe if you've got some time and a decent kitchen, whether it's on the road (a great 'thank you' breakfast for whoever's floor you just crashed on), or for a family Thanksgiving feast. My grandma loves this one."
— JACKIE MUSICK

INGREDIENTS:

1 medium-sized sweet potato

2 cups flour

3 teaspoons baking powder

1 teaspoon salt

$1/4$ cup ($1/2$ stick) margarine (softened or melted)

$3/4$ cup soy milk

1 teaspoon balsamic vinegar

1. Preheat oven to 450°F.
2. Put a pot of water over high heat. Peel the sweet potato and chop roughly. When water comes to a boil, add the chopped potato and boil until nice and soft—for about 5–8 minutes.
3. In a large bowl, sift or mix the flour, baking powder, and salt.
4. Measure and mix the soy milk and balsamic vinegar.
5. Add soy milk and vinegar mixture to the dry ingredients along with the margarine and mix together (you may have to knead it all together with yer hands and add a little more flour along the way. You want to end up with a dough that is sticky but not visibly wet).
6. Strain the potatoes and cool them under a stream of cold water. Then mash them up in a bowl (or use the same pot you boiled 'em in to save dishes).
7. Fold mashed sweet potatoes into dough using your hands. The dough will become very sticky at this point, so you may want to add just a little bit more flour.
8. Roll the dough out to about 1/2-inch thick on a well-floured cutting board or countertop (if you don't have a rolling pin, use last night's forty bottle). Using a cookie cutter or thin drinking glass, cut out yer biscuits and put them on a greased cookie sheet.
9. Cook for 12–18 minutes or until the bottoms are browned, but not burned.
10. If you haven't finished yer gravy yet, turn off the oven but leave the biscuits in there so they stay warm.

Makes 6–9 large biscuits.

VEGAN VEGETABLE GRAVY

"This recipe has endless variations in spicing and ingredients, but this is a good starting point. It should be chunky and flavorful, and it goes well on just about anything. I once lived for a week off a batch of this and a bag of bagels. Feeds at least five hungry people." —JACKIE MUSICK

1/2 cup unbleached white flour

1/4 cup nutritional yeast (also called brewer's yeast)

1/4 cup olive oil and a little bit more

Lots of water

1/4 cup tamari or soy sauce

1 1/2 teaspoons balsamic vinegar

A splash of Bragg Liquid Aminos, if you've got it

5–10 cloves garlic (crushed or minced)

Cumin, turmeric, oregano (all to taste), and a very small dash of cayenne pepper and curry powder.*

Black pepper (to taste)

1 medium-sized onion (chopped)

1 small head broccoli (broken into small pieces)

6–8 small white mushrooms (sliced)*

1/2 avocado (cut into slices or small cubes)*

DIRECTIONS:

1. In a dry wok or large skillet, brown (but don't burn!) the flour over a medium heat. The flour should change from off-white to a slightly darker golden-brown color. Do this slowly 'cause the flour burns easily and if it does, you'll have to start over.

2. Remove from heat and mix in nutritional yeast.

3. Add yer 1/4 cup of olive oil and mix well. Resulting mixture should be a brown, crumbly substance that looks kind of like oily dirt-clods (sounds kind of gross, but you'll see what I mean).

4. Return to a low-medium heat and add water while mixing constantly (if you have a wire whisk, use that) until mixture reaches a desirable consistency (not watery, but not gluey, either). This should take approximately 2 cups of water, but if you add too much, don't worry, just raise the heat a bit and boil off the excess liquid.

5. Add tamari or soy sauce, vinegar, (Bragg's), and garlic. Bring down to a low heat.

*Note: Any kind of vegetables and spices can be used in this gravy. These are just suggestions that I have found to work the best. Obviously, you should use what you like, whatever you've got lying around, or what you were able to Dumpster.

6. Add spices to taste. I usually use mainly cumin, turmeric, oregano, and lots of black pepper, but anything will do. The sooner you spice this, though, and the longer it sits on the stove, the more flavorful it will be.

7. Let simmer for about 5–10 minutes, adding water slowly if consistency becomes too thick (you don't have to do this, but it lets the spices set in).

8. In a separate skillet, sauté the chopped onion in a little bit of olive oil until brown. Throw it in the gravy.

9. Add vegetables, allowing appropriate cooking times for each (i.e., carrots or broccoli will take much longer than mushrooms or tomatoes).

10. Just before serving, mix in the avocado (if you've got it), adjust the spicing, and add or boil off water to adjust consistency.

Serve over a biscuit in a bowl, on a heap of mashed potatoes, or eat by itself as a meal.

Serves 5 or more.

from Michael Dahlquist

CHEESY SLEAZY

Silkworm's warm and noisy indie rock sound was quieted in the summer of 2005 when the band lost their drummer, Michael Dahlquist, in a fatal car accident. If you talk to anybody who knew Mikey, you'll be hard-pressed to find someone with lukewarm feelings about him—the general consensus is that he was an inspiration to everyone he encountered. Even his recipe (which was dreamed up with bandmate Andy Cohen) might inspire you to stay out a little later, order another round, make your way to the after-party, and maybe strike up a conversation with the pretty little thing you've been eyeing all night—because whatever happens tonight, Cheesy Sleazy will cure you tomorrow. Your hangover doesn't stand a chance against it—especially if you split it with one of your best pals. Here's to a heaven that's well-stocked with eggs, cheddar cheese, giant drum sets, and plenty of refried beans.

"About ten years ago, Andy and I lived across the street from each other in Seattle. On weekend mornings, he'd come over for what we called 'Cheesy Sleazy.' It's not a very complicated meal, but it's a huge and delicious meal. It's been a while since I made it, and I want it now." —MICHAEL DAHLQUIST

INGREDIENTS:

an onion, some red or green peppers,
    maybe some sausage and other stuff
    to throw in there, if you've got it
two cans of refried beans

Cheddar cheese
6 eggs
4 pieces of toast

DIRECTIONS:

1. In a wide, deep pan, sauté your onions, peppers, sausage, etc. until they're cooked all to hell.
2. Dump in the refried beans, and stir.

3. Cover the beans with slices of cheddar cheese, and cover the pan with a lid.

4. Fry the eggs over easy or sunny-side up (3 per person).

5. Toast the toast.

6. Place the 2 pieces of toast on a plate. Put the eggs on the toast. Then dump the Cheesy Sleazy on top of the eggs (half the pan per person).

Then you eat. It's a lot like *huevos rancheros*, only there's toast, and far more food than one should ever eat on a Sunday morning.

Really, this is only meant to serve 2.

from Mor Mor (Swedish for "Mother's Mother")

VARLDENS BASTA PANNKAKA

Smoosh was born when Death Cab for Cutie's Jason McGerr started giving drum lessons to an eleven-year-old named Chloe (whose last name will be revealed when she's a little older). Chloe was a natural, and soon her thirteen-year-old sister, Asya, who'd taken a few piano lessons, started kicking out some keyboard parts. Before long, the talented little duo was opening for the likes of Death Cab, Sleater-Kinney, and Sufjan Stevens.

When I ran into Smoosh's dad at a loud club in Austin and told him that we got a publisher for this cookbook, he exclaimed to the sisters Smoosh, "Girls, guess what—Grandma's *Varldens Basta Pannkaka* is going to be world famous!" Asya and Chloe seemed to look at him skeptically, but maybe they just couldn't hear him over the band—they smiled shyly when I handed them some earplugs. Dad assured me that it's one of their favorite recipes, and that it's been passed down along their Swedish lines. I'm not sure how to pronounce the name of it, but it's sort of a German Pancake or Dutch Baby. This big, custardy breakfast treat can be served with fruit, dusted with confectioners' sugar, or doused with syrup or jam.

INGREDIENTS:

2 cups flour

3/4 cup sugar

1 teaspoon baking powder

1 teaspoon vanilla sugar or extract

4 cups milk

2 eggs

6 tablespoons margarine or butter, melted

DIRECTIONS:

1. Preheat oven to 390°F. Grease a 9" x 13" baking pan.
2. Mix all ingredients, adding melted margarine or butter last.

3. Pour mixture into the prepared baking pan and place the pan low in the oven (bottom rack) for 45 minutes. When golden brown and puffed around the edges, remove from oven and serve immediately.

Serves 6.

SOUPS, SIDES, AND STARTERS | TWO

A LOT OF BEGINNER cooks foolishly believe that appetizers and side dishes are unnecessary, but these are the extras that will enhance your whole entertaining experience. Think of them as your light show, your smoke machine, or your hype man. They're the finishing touches that show you're ready to party, and there's a dish in this chapter to improve every occasion.

Here, you'll find some perfect party fare, whether you're serving cocktails or just cracking open some beers. Ditch the Doritos and offer some of Craig Wedren's simple Baked Brie, fry up Pegasuses-XL's killer potato pancakes, or throw together Sorry About Dresden's aptly titled Life of the Party Chicken on a Stick. For an even simpler snack, buy a bag of tortilla chips and pair them with the Descendents' *Pico de Gallo* or the guacamole from Viva Voce—who've also shared their recipe for hot and spicy boiled peanuts.

If you're going all out for a gourmet dinner party, whet your guests' appetites with a foodie favorite, like Battles' decadent roasted bone marrow, Scoville Unit's Spanish tortillas, or Headlights' fun and fancy crab Rangoon. Alternatively, if you're just whipping up supper for your nearest-and-dearest, don't you think your roommate/loved one deserves a vegetable with that George Foreman–grilled chicken? Put that frozen corn back into the freezer right now. You need to try Komakino's mushy peas (which are better than any I've tasted in London fish-and-chips shops), Birds of Avalon's Asian-influenced Not-So-Greasy Greens, the Rosebuds' cheesy zucchini boats, or Edie Sedgwick's easy brussels sprouts.

Any of the soups—the Black Hollies' fiery lentil soup, Brakes' veggie puree, Mojave 3's comforting Leek & Potato Soup, and Enon's adorable Recipe for the One Who Is Getting Some Kind of Cold—can be served as a meal, but they also pair nicely with a sandwich for a casual dinner party. It's hard to screw up a soup, and the homemade varieties taste so much better than their canned counterparts. They'll totally impress your guests, and isn't that the point here? After all, the goal of any host or hostess is similar to the ambition of a touring band—to develop a hungry fan base who'll rave about you and always come back for more.

from Ian Williams

ROASTED BONE MARROW "BATTLES STYLE"

New York's Battles is something of an instrumental rock super-group. While Ian Williams (of Don Caballero), David Konopka (of Lynx), and avant-jazz composer Tyondai Braxton create otherworldly noises, drummer John Stanier (of Helmet and Tomahawk) plays with his ride cymbal about seven feet in the air, so in the middle of his stuttering off-time beats, he can stand up and bash it with added drama. When it comes to food, they're a little more down-to-earth. "Food is one of the most intimate things in life—we put it into our bodies every day," says Ian. "So make an effort to get to know it, as well as those who provide it for you—your local butchers, farmers, and bakers." Since you're going to need some cow bones and duck skin for this recipe, having a good relationship with your butcher will certainly ease the food-shopping process. Eating marrow may sound a little creepy to the uninitiated, but it's actually a savory wintertime delicacy. Check out the recipe-within-a-recipe for homemade potato chips.

"Note before starting: Cooking is an art and we don't really believe in recipes. Food, like music, depends largely on its ingredients and how they play off of each other—blend or clash—to create the final experience. Each time we cook and each time we play, the ingredients are a little different and so is the result. Although we are essentially giving you a recipe, please approach it with thought and make adjustments as you please. It may taste and feel better that way. We like to call this 'Drunk Rabbit, Blended Smooth with a Straw' or 'Roasted Bone Marrow "Battles Style."'

"Bones are the basics of cooking, particularly for all those amazing heartwarming 'comfort food' dishes—soups, stews, braises—they are what stocks are made out of and what enriches sauces. Bone marrow is the vehicle that transports all the great flavor and what gives different dishes their lip-smacking quality. To appreciate food, one needs to understand and appreciate bones. And like much great music, bones are rather neglected. This recipe will list ingredients for a single serving for four people, though you may find yourself eventually eating it all yourself." —IAN WILLIAMS

4 veal or beef marrow bones (ask that the bones be cut into 3"–4" pieces from the center portion of the leg—that is where you get the best and most marrow from)

Sea salt

1 piece of skin from duck breast

1 russet potato

Canola oil

1 tomato (or a 14-ounce can of whole tomatoes, when not in season)

Fleur de sel

3 cloves of fresh garlic

A bit of curly parsley

1 loaf of hearth-baked bread

PREPARATION:

BONES

1. Put the bones into a bowl and cover with cold water. Add 2 tablespoons of sea salt and put in the fridge to soak for at least 12 hours. Change the water every 3 hours and each time add salt to the new water. This will remove any traces of blood from the bones.

2. When ready to cook, drain the water and dry the bones with a rag. Preheat the oven to 450°F and lightly oil a roasting pan. Roast the bones for about 20 minutes. When done, the center of the marrow should be warm and it should puff up slightly.

CONDIMENTS

1. Take a piece of duck skin (with some fat) and cut it into 1" x 3" pieces. If you are friendly with your butcher, he will give it to you for free, because of all those silly people who want their breasts skinless.

2. Warm up a skillet and put the skin "fat side down" on low to low-medium heat. The skin will crisp up slowly while cooking. Feel free to press down while cooking, to evenly cook the surface of the skin. Turn when one side becomes golden brown and cook until both sides are this color. This may take 15–20 minutes.

3. Cut the potato into approximately $1/8$"-thick slices. Get a pot of salted water boiling and dunk them in there for 20 seconds to remove some starch from the outside.

4. Get the canola oil to about 325°F in a frying pan and place the potato slices in it. Lightly salt when done. This is a trial and error process—you may have to play with the thickness of potato slices and the heat of the oil, but once you get it down, they come out great! Also, you can add the duck fat from crisping up the duck skin to your canola oil for flavor. It does not suck.

5. Take a tomato and dice finely. Salt lightly with a little bit of *fleur de sel*, add a touch of canola oil, and mix it up.

6. Take 3 cloves of garlic and dice finely.

CONSUMPTION:

1. Take the four bones and arrange on a plate. Top the bones with a generous amount of *fleur de sel*.

2. Surround one bone with minced garlic.

3. Top the next one with crispy duck skin.

4. Let the third bone sit in a pool of tomatoes.

5. And surround the last bone with potato chips.

6. Garnish with some curly parsley.

7. Serve with a basket of toasted bread.

I like to take a piece of country bread, dig up marrow from the bone, and spread it all over . . . then top it with as much raw garlic as I can, and add salt if necessary.

John likes to take a piece of duck skin and top it with bone marrow and *fleur de sel*. He enjoys a taste and follows it with a bite of bread and a sip of Shiraz to de-clog his veins.

Dave likes to look at his plate for a few minutes . . . marvel (with the critical eye of a designer) at how much it resembles blood and bones. Then he takes a piece of country bread and spreads the bone marrow and *fleur de sel* over it. Tops it with chopped tomato and enjoys.

Ty likes to take a potato chip and top it with bone marrow. He adds *fleur de sel* and tops with another piece of potato chip to make a mini–potato-and-marrow sandwich.

Serves 4.

from Cheetie Kumar

NOT-SO-GREASY GREENS

Cheetie Kumar, a guitar and culinary goddess, is known for her formidable solos and enviable culinary skills. After playing with North Carolina's the Cherry Valence for years, she and bandmate/husband, Paul Siler, left the band to start Birds of Avalon, a straight-up rock 'n' roll four-piece. Cheetie was born in India, raised in the Bronx, and has adopted Raleigh, North Carolina, as her current home, and her meatless, grease-free greens have international appeal. They're a healthy alternative to the collards typically served with Southern home cookin', but the flavors of ginger, cumin, and coriander make them a nice side for South Asian fare, as well.

"It was only after I moved to North Carolina that I realized a plate of soul food does not live up to its name without a heapin' mess o' collard greens (or turnip greens or kale). This Southern tradition started with the arrival of African slaves to the cotton fields of the region. They were given food left over from the plantation house, which included the tops of turnips and other greens, pigs' feet, ham hocks, and other meat scraps. Out of necessity, and perhaps nostalgia for the one-pot stews common in West African cooking, the method of boiling tough greens with a ham hock for hours became a part of the Southern kitchen.

"A pot of greens—stinky as they are—and its 'liquor' (the broth) sopped up with a stack of Johnny cakes, hoe cakes, or hot cornbread, is so loved that it's been sung about by everyone from Peg Leg Sam to James Brown and the JBs—all of whom have no doubt been starved for a good meal somewhere far from home cooking.

"I don't pretend that the following recipe can live up to this legend. One roadside produce peddler in Pender County stepped aside and asked the Lord to strike me down when I told him I was going to sauté my greens—not boil 'em all day. But if you, like me, avoid the swine (aka *seasoning* in the South), you gotta do something to give back flavor lost without the meat. I choose Asian ingredients.

"This dish is an important part of a vegetable plate—good with rice and beans or as a side dish for fish or chicken or whatever. And it doesn't take hours to make." —CHEETIE KUMAR

3–4 pounds (2 bunches) collard greens or
   2–3 pounds kale or spinach (the
   spinach really mellows out the flavor)
1 large yellow onion
One 2-inch piece of ginger
6–8 medium cloves garlic
2 tablespoons olive oil
1 tablespoon ground cumin*

1 tablespoon ground coriander*
1 teaspoon red pepper flakes
salt and pepper
1 beer (12 oz.—whatever kind you like)
2 tablespoons soy sauce
1/3 cup apple cider vinegar
1–2 tablespoons honey
3 shredded carrots
1 tablespoon sesame oil, olive oil, or butter

DIRECTIONS:

1. Fill a big bowl or clean sink with cool water and throw in the collard greens or kale. Shake the greens around in the water to loosen any dirt while they are soaking. Tear the tough ribs from the middle of the leaves and discard.

2. Put the trimmed leaves in a colander or bowl. If you are using kale, drain and replace the water from the bowl or sink and wash one more time. The curly kale leaves trap a lot more dirt than the flat collard leaves . . . and gritty greens are no good.

3. Coarsely chop and set aside.

4. Slice the onion.

5. Peel and finely chop the ginger and garlic.

6. Heat a large skillet or wok over medium-high heat. Add the olive oil. Sauté the onions and ginger until the onions are translucent (about 5–6 minutes).

7 Add the garlic, stir for 20–30 seconds—until the garlic is fragrant but not brown.

8. Add the cumin, coriander, and red pepper flakes.

9. Stir well for a few seconds until the mixture is fragrant. Add the greens, and toss (tongs work best).

*If possible, use whole cumin seeds and coriander seeds. Toast them in a dry, hot skillet, shaking constantly till fragrant. Cool and grind in a spice mill or mortar and pestle. If using ground spices, make sure they are fresh (not more than 6 months old).

10. Season with salt and pepper and cover for a few minutes till the greens have wilted. Don't worry if it seems like the pan is too small—the greens cook down quite a bit. Throw them into the pan in batches, if necessary.

11. Add in beer, soy sauce, apple cider vinegar, and honey.

12. Stir, bring to a boil, cover, and reduce the heat to medium. Cook for 5–10 minutes, till the greens are almost tender.

13. Add the shredded carrots.

14. Replace cover and cook for another 5–10 minutes—until all the flavors are incorporated. Check for salt. If you like more of a vinegar bite, add another 1–2 tablespoons vinegar and cook another minute.

15. Finish the dish with 1 tablespoon toasted sesame oil, olive oil, or butter, whatever your preference.

Serves 4–6.

from Justin Angelo Morey

"HAVE MERCY ON ME" LENTIL SOUP

If you're one of those kids who feels like you were born twenty-five or thirty years too late and now have to settle for live recordings of shows you should have attended in the mid-'60s, I feel your pain. Reunion tours will only disappoint you, and cover bands will make you cringe, but all you latter-day mods do have one beacon of hope—the Black Hollies. These guys bring on the party with freak-out blues-rock that channels the British Invasion and seduces hipster girls into dancing around with tambourines. Singer Justin Angelo Morey, an avid cook with a solid record collection, uses vinyl to time his recipes. (You'll be able to make his lentil soup without the help of a record player, but it won't be nearly as much fun.) He does offer a warning about his cooking style, though. "Some people think I make things a little too hot," Justin admits, as his British wife, Loz, nods gravely at his side. "I cook all the time for my wife, and she often says things like, 'My arse is on fire,' or 'I think you like to watch other people suffer.' I can't help it, though. I just love spicy food." If you're unsure about how spicy you like your soup, start with just a pinch of the crushed red pepper and the cayenne, and add more to taste as the soup simmers.

"Although the majority of my dining is spent at various overly expensive restaurants in the Jersey City area (like my favourite of all, the Flamingo on Montgomery and Greene Street), sometimes the royalty checks arrive rather tardy. This leaves the wife and I to suss out other means to get through the day or a couple of months, as the case may be. This recipe can get you through the tough times that we are all subjected to every now and again. I find that the key to this soup is adding a bit of your soul. Use only high-end ingredients when you're having guests over for a munch, and you can sit back knowing that, hell, if the bills don't get paid off this month, at least a compliment or two should be thrown in your direction before the power officially gets turned off." —JUSTIN ANGELO MOREY

1/4 cup extra-virgin olive oil

1 large onion (dice half and chop the other half)

kosher salt, to taste

crushed black pepper, to taste

2 teaspoons crushed red pepper (use less if you can't take the heat)

3 stalks of celery (chopped)

3 carrots (chopped)

2 cloves of garlic (minced)

1 cup of cauliflower (chopped)

2 teaspoons curry powder

1 teaspoon cumin

16-ounce bag dry lentils

14.5-ounce tin organic roasted garlic vegetable broth (any vegetable broth will do—but look for one that is low in salt)

14.5-ounce tin whole peeled tomatoes

8 cups water

2 teaspoons cayenne pepper (use one—or less—if you are weak)

1 large soup pot with lid

1 wooden spoon

1 John Mayall and the Bluesbreakers LP (the one with Eric Clapton)

1 Fleetwood Mac (with Peter Green) *Black Magic Woman* double LP

1 Beatles *Revolver* LP

1. Put on side 1 of the Bluesbreakers LP. Hell yeah. Nice version of that tune originally done by Otis Rush, isn't it? You're gonna be well fed by the time this soup is done simmering.

2. Pour 1/4 cup of extra virgin olive oil into a large pot over low to medium heat. Add onion, salt, black pepper, and crushed red pepper. Place lid on top of pot. Simmer for roughly 6 minutes, or until onions are clear and soft.

3. Add celery, carrots, garlic, cauliflower, curry, and cumin, and stir. Place lid back on and let simmer for 10 minutes, occasionally using the wooden spoon to mix it up a bit.

4. Turn record over to side 2.

5. Add lentils, vegetable broth, and whole peeled tomatoes (juice included). Stir, breaking up the tomatoes with your wooden spoon, and place lid on top again. Let simmer for another 10 minutes, stirring occasionally.

6. Add 8 cups of water and increase to high heat, and leave uncovered until it begins to boil.

7. Put on side 1 of the first record from Fleetwood Mac's *Black Magic Woman* double LP. (I solely acknowledge Peter Green's Fleetwood Mac as the one and only Fleetwood Mac.)

8. When the soup begins to boil, reduce heat to a very low setting. Add cayenne pepper. Stir. Place lid back on.

9. Let simmer for at least 2 hours, at the very minimum. You may have to add some more water because as the hard lentils transform into soft, delightful legumes, they shall absorb a lot of liquid. This is now going to be the waiting period that will feel like forever, but in fact will be worth every single minute. Have some red wine. Pour yourself a pint of Belgian lager. Play sides 2, 3, and 4 of the *Black Magic Woman* double LP. Listen to how amazing they were, before they got taken over by a pair of singer-songwriters from California.

10. When lentils are officially finished cooking, put on side 1 of the Beatles' *Revolver* LP. Serve yourself a bowl of lentil soup and hope that the record doesn't stop playing on account of the electric bill being overdue. Cheers.

Serves 6.

from Marc Beatty

HEALTHY GREEN SOUP

Brakes, who hail from Brighton, are a little more punk rock than Editors and Bloc Party, but with infectious tracks like "All Night Disco Party," they ignite the same kind of barroom dance-offs as their Brit rock brethren. Before Brakes formed, front man Eamon Hamilton was the keyboardist for British Sea Power, and bassist Marc Beatty spent his days running a rehearsal and recording space called Mockin' Bird Studio, where Brakes recorded their first single. Packed with cabbage and broccoli, Marc's Healthy Green Soup is infinitely more nourishing than Shonen Knife's so-called Healthy Green Tea Cookies (which are delicious, if not nutritious). Marc is also the only recipe contributor who reminds us that cleanliness is next to godliness in the kitchen—whether you're degerming your hands or de-skanking your broccoli.

"This basic soup is easy to make and can also be used as a template for more adventurous creations. It's a good way to get rid of leftover vegetables and is very good for you. The ingredients in this soup are my preference but you can improvise and use whatever you like really." —MARC BEATTY

INGREDIENTS:

3 bits of garlic (cloves, that is)

1 large onion

1 potato, scrubbed

Half a savoy cabbage

1 leek

1 whole bunch of broccoli

5 cups of water

4 tablespoons butter ($1/2$ a stick)

salt and pepper

$1/2$ cup of cheese (cheddar is fine, Parmesan or Gruyère also work well)

$1/2$ teaspoon ground cumin

a sprinkling of chili flakes

1. First, WASH YER HANDS! Then wash and chop up the vegetables, as follows: Finely chop the garlic and onion. Set aside in a bowl. Chop the potato in half and then into quarters and slice from there. Shred the cabbage. Chop the end off the leek and then slice the white part into inch-thick chunks. Place the potato, cabbage, and leek in a separate bowl. De-floret the broccoli and put the florets aside, in a third bowl. Take the broccoli stalk and remove any skanky bits. Now chop off the bottom and then chop the whole de-skanked stalk into thick chunks.

2. Boil the water in a saucepan and add the broccoli stalk with a pinch of salt, and turn heat down to let it simmer. After about 10 minutes, add the cabbage, leek, and potato to the saucepan with the broccoli stalk, turn the heat back up, and boil all together for another 10 minutes. The vegetables should be submerged in water—add a little more if you need to.

3. In the meantime, melt butter in a large, deep frying pan and add the onion and garlic, frying lightly.

4. Once the 10 minutes is up, drain the vegetables, but keep the water, as this is your stock. The broccoli stalk should be very soft. Add the boiled vegetables to the frying pan with the onion and garlic. Turn the heat up a bit and give it all a good frying for about 5 minutes, stirring frequently.

5. Once the potato is a little browned, add the stock. Now, add the broccoli florets, and simmer the whole lot together for just under 10 minutes, adding salt and pepper to taste.

6. While that's bubbling away, grate your cheese onto a plate. When almost 10 minutes have passed, take the pan off the heat and give the whole thing a whizz with one of those handheld blenders or let it cool for a few minutes, and then carefully pour it into a food processor to puree it.

7. Once the mixture is fully liquefied, return it to a very low heat, and add the cheese and half a teaspoon of ground cumin. Stir it all in until the cheese has melted.

8. Give the soup a light sprinkling of chili flakes, and add more salt and pepper if needed.

9. Serve in bowls with a generous chunk of slightly toasted crusty bread on the side.

Serves 4.

from Craig Wedren himself

BAKED BRIE

Craig Wedren's old band, Shudder to Think, was part of the Washington, DC, hardcore scene, but his unmistakable voice, which has often been compared to Freddie Mercury's, made them stand out among their Dischord label mates. Since the band's unraveling, Wedren has concentrated on his solo work, composed music for film (he scored the Jack-Black-as-music-teacher vehicle *School of Rock*), and formed Baby, an eclectic dance-party band that features his dramatic vocals over synthetic '80s beats. But at the end of the day, this man just wants him some baked Brie. This recipe is the perfect thing to throw together before a last-minute get-together—it couldn't be simpler or more irresistible.

> "Here is my current (no pun intended) fave recipe. I can't take credit for it on account of I barely cook, and when I do it's a recipe called 'Fridge-dregs-improv,' where I make something new out of whatever's in the apartment that doesn't need pesty 'ingredients' or high-falutin 'ovens.' BUT this Baked Brie recipe is from The Lady Meggan Lennon, and when she makes it, I die of pleasure."
>
> —CRAIG WEDREN

INGREDIENTS:

One 8-inch wheel Brie cheese

One 12-ounce jar of jam (any flavor will do, but apricot is fantastic)

1/4 cup dried cherries

1/4 cup sliced toasted almonds

Plenty of French bread

DIRECTIONS:

1. Preheat oven to 350°F.
2. Put the entire wheel of Brie in an 8-inch tart or pie dish.
3. Using a warmed sharp knife, slice the top rind off of the Brie.

4. Stud the dried cherries equally spaced throughout in the Brie, pushing them about halfway down.

5. Spread the jam on top, covering the entire wheel of Brie, then sprinkle almonds on top of jam.

5. Bake for 35 minutes. Slather on freshly sliced French bread.

Serves 8–10.

from Bill Stevenson

BILL'S *PICO DE GALLO*

"I have a title for the cookbook," my friend Brian said, as he handed me a PBR and slid onto the stool beside me at a grimy dive bar in Greensboro, North Carolina. "'I Like Food, Food Tastes Good'—you know, from the Descendents song?" I'd like to propose a toast to Brian Bedsworth because he not only came up with the title, but he's also responsible for tracking down a bunch of the recipes. This book wouldn't exist without him. We were so excited when Bill Stevenson, drummer for the legendary LA spaz-punk four-piece (who also was Black Flag's drummer in the early '80s and who is now a member of the most recent incarnation of Evan Dando's Lemonheads) gave us the okay to use the title. He also sent this fresh and fantastic *pico de gallo* recipe—which he always makes for bands who are staying at his house when they pass through town, or when bands are recording at his studio, the Blasting Room, in Fort Collins, Colorado.

INGREDIENTS:

7 roma tomatoes

2 jalapeños

some garlic salt

a bunch of cilantro

1 white onion

1 lime

DIRECTIONS:

1. dice everything up real small
2. i use scissors on the cilantro—use maybe 1/2 the bunch
3. squeeze about 1/2 of the lime in there
4. throw it all in a bowl and stir it up
5. try some with chips—adjust the garlic salt to taste
6. it tastes better after it sits for a while

Makes about 2 cups.

from Edie herself

BRUSSELS SPROUTS À LA DENZEL WASHINGTON

Edie Sedgwick was a waif-ish Warhol superstar who died of a drug overdose in 1971. This recipe comes from her transgendered reincarnate, who writes electro-trash odes to famous folks like Christian Slater, Martin Sheen, Lucy Liu, and Haley Joel Osment. Like Edie's sharp-witted songs and the hilarious celebrity-inspired haikus on her MySpace page, this simple brussels sprouts recipe conveys Edie's fantabulous knack for elevating movie story-lines and Hollywood gossip into comedic art.

INGREDIENTS:

10–12 large brussels sprouts (none of those sad little wilted baby balls, dahling!)

1 tablespoon soy margarine (or butter, for those who prefer a sinful dab o' dairy)

Salt and pepper, to taste (for me, the spicier the better—and not just in the realm of brussels-sprout preparation)

GUSTATORY MANIFESTO:

If you know me, you know I love celebrities. I surround myself with them. They are the center of my life and art, my *raison d'être*, my sun, my moon, my sweet Kung Pao, and General Tso all rolled into one. At a party, you'll find me gossiping with Jack Nicholson or Madge, never with a lowly valet or server of *hors d'oeuvres* (unless, of course, he is particularly handsome and has something he'd like to show me in the pantry). The night tables of my boudoir are slathered with *People* magazine and *Entertainment Weekly*. My living will stipulates that, should I require life support after a tragic accident, I not be resuscitated unless I can be wheeled into the taping of a *Friends* reunion at a major network studio.

Because I am obsessed with fame in this way, I incorporate celebrities into every facet of my day. Food preparation and consumption are no different. The day often begins with me staring into two blubbery discs of yolk in my sunny-side up eggs (the "Pam Anderson") with a long stick of sausage on the side (the "Tommy Lee"). For an energy jolt around lunch I'll have a "Jodie Foster" (the unforgettable peanut-butter/jam/sugar sandwich she chomps in *Taxi Driver*). A simple dinner before heading to the studio might be the "Cheech Marin" (rice and beans) or a functional, if generic, "James Gandolfini" (pasta and red sauce). When I binge on sweets, specifically chocolate, I consider that I am "Gumping." When I starve myself in preparation for a show, I am "Olsoning" for the day. You get the idea.

My quick-and-dirty brussels sprouts recipe honors Academy Award winner Denzel Washington and, more specifically, his incredible performance in Spike Lee's film *Malcolm X*. Let me "break it down":

DIRECTIONS:

1. Wash the surface of your sprouts thoroughly under hot water, tearing off any brown, wilted leaves. The Islamic tradition celebrates clean foods (and the rejection of the white man's "dirty swine"). What person—Christian, Muslim, Jew, Buddhist, or Jain—wants to eat rotten vegetables, anyway?

2. Chop the hard, stubby end off of each individual sprout.

3. Mark the end of each sprout with an "X." This "X" allows the steam to thoroughly penetrate the sprouts and pays tribute to a great performance by a man some call the greatest actor of his generation.

4. Get that vegetable steamer you bought at Ikea that time with a gift certificate out of the cupboard and remember how it works. While doing so, recognize how much better Denzel was in *Malcolm X* than in *Training Day*.

5. Steam the sprouts until you can easily spear them with a fork, but do not overcook! Ten minutes maximum is a good rule of thumb. You should also remove the lid for a moment after the first minute to release some of the sprouts' smelly methane. The gas will dissipate much as Malcolm's hatred for white devils dissipated after his pilgrimage to Mecca.

6. Season the sprouts with margarine, salt, and pepper. You're done—but will remember the struggle for freedom in each savory bite's bitter aftertaste.

Serves 2-3,
depending on how much you love brussels sprouts
(and Denzel Washington).

from Toko Yasuda

A RECIPE FOR THE ONE WHO IS GETTING
SOME KIND OF COLD

Toko Yasuda, of the Brooklyn- and Philly-based pop trio Enon, is responsible for some seriously cute vocals, as well as this endearing soup recipe. It's a spicy version of the basic miso soup served in Japanese restaurants, and it's perfect for clearing the sinuses or warding off an impending cold. If you're feeling under the weather, a cup of this soup is the perfect serving size, but it also works as a comforting appetizer that packs a gingery and garlicky punch.

> "This is the SOUP i make when i am coming down on something chilling . . . . . it takes about 20 minutes to make."
> —TOKO YASUDA

INGREDIENTS:

A pinch of seaweed for broth (optional—u can get the powder or dried kombu seaweed at Japanese supermarkets or Asian markets)

Tofu ($1/2$ a package of Silk brand) (cut in small cubes)

Ginger (a lot of them) (cut into very small pieces)

Garlic (a lot of them) (garlic press them)

Miso paste (to taste)

Scallion (chop it)

Salt, pepper, and cayenne pepper (to taste)

DIRECTIONS:

1. in a pot, boil some water (about a cup) with a pinch of seaweed stuff. . . .
2. when water starts to boil, add tofu, and $2/3$ of ginger, and $1/3$ of garlic which u prepared.

3. lower the heat, add miso (if u are not sure how much miso u wanna add, add little by little until it tastes good to u . . .).

4. add scallions and the rest of the garlic and ginger.

5. add salt, pepper, and cayenne pepper, for the extra flavor.

Please eat it when it is hot! u should feel the zzzzzzzz . . . . feeling on your throat with ginger and garlic, and i hope u are sweating. Ideally, u are going to bed with this Soup Buzz.

Serves 1.

from Tristan Wraight

ROCK 'N' ROLL RANGOON

When I first met Tristan Wraight, he was touring with Maserati. He added a fuzzed-out sound to the instrumental quartet's set then, and now his shoegazey style finds its way into the live shows of his current project, Headlights—a perpetually touring pop trio with dreamy boy-girl vocals. Their songs are so bouncy and pleasant, and co-vocalist Erin Fein's voice is so clear and sweet that sometimes I just want to hug their CD. Even their recipe comes out looking totally cute—if you can find eggroll wrappers or very large wonton wrappers. All I could find in my supermarket's freezer were really small wonton wrappers, so I couldn't fit much filling in them or fashion them into "little bags of gold," as Tristan suggests. I just folded them in half like dumplings, though, and they were devoured too quickly for anyone to marvel at their design, anyway. Also, while I'm sure they're great with fresh crabmeat, I used the very economical canned variety from the tuna fish aisle and the filling was delicious.

INGREDIENTS:

8 ounce container (or 1 cup) of cream
 cheese

1 or 2 cloves of fresh garlic

a knuckle-sized piece of fresh ginger root

half of one small shallot

a bunch of fresh chive stems

3/4 cup crabmeat (imitation or real)

1/4 teaspoon soy sauce

2 egg yolks

2 tablespoons milk

1 package of eggroll wrappers or the
 largest wonton wrappers you can find

vegetable oil

plum sauce or sweet-and-sour sauce
 (optional)

1. Take a cup of cream cheese and put it in a mixing bowl.
2. Peel and finely chop the garlic, ginger, and shallot, and then finely chop 5 chive stems. Only use a knuckle-sized piece of ginger because it's very strong.
3. Put them in the mixing bowl.
4. Break up and chop the crabmeat and add that to the mix.
5. Add a quarter of a teaspoon of soy sauce.
6. Mix well with a fork.

EGG WASH

1. Beat two egg yolks and add two tablespoons of milk in a small bowl. Whisk it up.

PUT IT TOGETHER:

1. Open the package of wonton wrappers and separate them. Take one wrapper and dip it in the egg wash.
2. Put a tablespoon of the mix in the center of the wonton wrapper.
3. Fold up the corners and sides of the wrapper to make it like a sack and tie the tops of the corners together using a chive. It should look like a little bag of gold.
4. Repeat until mix is gone.

COOK IT:

1. Coat a non-stick frying pan with a quarter of an inch of vegetable oil.
2. Turn the flame on to medium so the oil gets hot. You can splash the oil with a little bit of water, if it pops when the water hits the oil, then you know the oil is hot enough.
3. Let each side get golden brown. Rotate as necessary. Once it is uniformly golden brown take it out of the pan and put it onto a plate that is covered with a paper towel to soak up the extra oil.
4. Give these puppies a little while to cool because they get really freakin' hot. Serve with a plum or sweet-and-sour sauce if you like. Enjoy!

Serves 6.

from Dennis Caswell

GARLIC MUSHY PEAS

Growing up, I really hated peas, but my little sister, Kyle, loved them so much that she would eat them frozen, right out of box. Sometimes, when we were watching TV together, she'd stare right at me and slowly pop a frozen pea into her mouth, as if it were the greatest delicacy on the face of the earth. Of course, I found this revolting, but not so revolting that I'd put down my bag of Sour Cream 'n' Onion Tato Skins, or anything. I guess it's not surprising that my svelte and beautiful sister is lying out on a beach right now in a string bikini, while I'm trying to talk you into dousing your peas with heavy cream. Seriously, though, this recipe from Brit-rockers Komakino may convert you into a lover of peas—and just in case you want to pronounce this recipe title in the proper British style, "mushy" rhymes with "slushy"—not "pushy." Recipe contributor and bass player Dennis Caswell, who sporadically writes a blog called Rock 'N' Roll Kitchen, says, "I absolutely love them. Admittedly they're not the healthiest, but my word, aren't they good?" Top your pile of peas with a broiled salmon filet, crack open a can of Boddingtons, and dinner is served.

"Mushy peas are pretty simple but quite unusual in the sense that people just don't make them at home. They normally come from the chip shop with too much salt added and artificial flourescent colouring! Not to mention, they don't come with garlic or balsamic." —DENNIS CASWELL

INGREDIENTS:

10 ounces frozen garden peas (boiled and drained)

1 clove garlic (finely chopped)

3 tablespoons good balsamic vinegar

3 tablespoons double (heavy) cream

1 tablespoon fresh parsley

Salt

1. Place the boiled peas in a saucepan and mash roughly with a potato masher (you could use a fork if you wanted), over medium heat.
2. Add the garlic and balsamic vinegar, stirring for 1 minute or so.
3. Add the cream, allowing it to bubble for a further minute.
4. Take off the heat and throw in some parsley and season to taste with salt.

    Very simple but really very good indeed.

Serves 3–4.

from Rachel Goswell

LEEK & POTATO SOUP

When the members of Slowdive unplugged their fuzzy guitars to form Mojave 3, they adopted a soft, serene, and mildly countrified sound that's reminiscent of Mazzy Star and the Cowboy Junkies. Neil Halstead and Rachel Goswell share vocals in the trio and they've both released solo records, as well. Together, they carry tunes that are as mellow and calming as this creamy soup.

> "My dad used to make this soup when I was little and this recipe endures throughout my family. Be sure to wash your leeks carefully, as they tend to hold a lot of sand."
>
> —RACHEL GOSWELL

INGREDIENTS:

2 tablespoons of butter

3 medium-sized leeks, chopped (white parts only)

3 medium-sized carrots, peeled and chopped

1 pound of potatoes, peeled and chopped

2 garlic cloves, crushed

a pinch of sugar

salt and pepper, to taste

4 cups of cold water

crusty bread (optional)

DIRECTIONS:

1. Melt the butter in a large soup pot, throw in chopped leeks, carrots, and potatoes and coat in the butter for around 5 minutes over medium heat.
2. Add in crushed garlic, sugar, salt, and pepper. Mix well.
3. Add in the water, bring to a boil, and simmer for around 20 minutes until all the vegetables are soft. Then carefully pour the hot soup into a blender and puree it (or use an

immersion blender to puree it right in the pot). This soup should be quite thick (thickness will depend on ratio of leeks to potatoes).

This is a real winter warmer and is great with some crusty bread! It will keep for a few days in an airtight container in the fridge. It only tends to last a day in my house, though, as it gets consumed pretty quickly!

Serves 4.

from Jeff's dad, Mel Tobias

THE SECRET TOBIAS FAMILY POTATO PANCAKE RECIPE

Imagine a trio of winged horses dive-bombing through the sky, and you'll get a sense of what Pegasuses-XL sounds like. Athens, Georgia's, heavy-duty rocket-fueled three-piece, often dressed in matching white hoodies, assaults audiences with pummeling drums, deranged keyboard parts, and caffeine-crazed lyrics. They're also very sweet people. I met their drummer, Mark Dale, years ago when he was touring with his old band, Disband, and I was faced with the challenge of cooking something that he'd be able to eat—he's both lactose-intolerant and gluten-intolerant, which means he can never eat pizza and, when ordering fast food on the road, he must forfeit his burger buns. (I'm not saying this to embarrass you, Mark; I'm just encouraging your fans to cook for you when you're on tour. By the way, ladies, he's 6'7", has a very kind disposition, and knows how to fly planes!) Anyway, these wheat- and dairy-free potato pancakes are Mark Dale–friendly, and also a tradition in the family of Jeff Tobias, who is not only a Pegasus, but also the singer for math-core quartet We Vs. the Shark. The recipe was kindly composed by the third Pegasus, Joel Hatstat, who is also a member of Cinemechanica and Contraband, the band that plays the Contra soundtrack while two players beat the game on 8-bit NES. (That's Nintendo Entertainment System, folks, and yes, it's as rad as it sounds.)

INGREDIENTS:

7–8 medium-sized old potatoes (approximately 2.5 pounds)

1 large onion, peeled

2 eggs

2 tablespoons potato flour (or you can use regular flour if you're gluten-tolerant)

1 tablespoon salt

1 teaspoon white pepper

Corn oil

Applesauce and/or sour cream (optional)

1. Peel all the potatoes and cover them w/ cold water until you are ready to make the pancakes, in order to keep them fresh.

2. Grate the potatoes and the onion alternately into a strainer that is suspended over another bowl—the onion juice will help prevent the potatoes from darkening. Using a wooden spoon, squeeze or press out as much liquid as possible from the mixture. You can also use yr hands. Reserve all liquid and let it settle in the bowl for 2 or 3 minutes.

3. Put the pressed potato-and-onion mixture aside in a clean bowl. Carefully pour off the watery part of the liquid but do not discard the thick, starchy paste at the bottom of the bowl. Scrape that into the potato mixture.

4. Add the eggs, potato flour, salt, and pepper and mix thoroughly.

5. Heat up about a $1/2$-inch-depth of oil in a heavy skillet and drop the potato mixture into the oil, roughly 2 tablespoons per pancake. Fry evenly on both sides to a golden brown.

6. Dry on paper towels and keep warm in an oven until serving—however, don't wait too long or they will get soggy.

The best side dish to go w/ potato pancakes is obviously applesauce. I will add that they are also the jam with sour cream.

Word.

Makes about 20 pancakes.

from Kelly Crisp

ZUCCHINI SLIPPERS

Who needs a honeymoon when you can spend your whole married life on tour? A week after their wedding in 2001, Kelly Crisp and Ivan Howard became the Rosebuds, and they've been splitting their time between the road and their Raleigh, North Carolina, home ever since. Armed with call-and-response pop sing-alongs, the energetic duo is often joined by a collective of musician friends. This recipe makes the most of an abundance of summer squash, and with the addition of different cheeses and spices, you can change it up all summer long. For a Tex-Mex variation, try subbing in a handful of cilantro for the basil, mix in some diced tomatoes or salsa, and replace the cheeses with *queso blanco* and Pepper Jack.

"This is a recipe we thought up because we keep a garden and zucchini and squash are always easy to grow and one plant produces so much. My favorite way to eat zucchini is sliced into circles, sautéed with olive oil, and sprinkled with sea salt. But, since we have so much of it, we came up with this casserole-like dish for something different."
—KELLY CRISP

INGREDIENTS:

4 zucchini and squash

12 fresh basil leaves, plus more for garnish

1/2 cup bread crumbs, plus more for sprinkling

1 tablespoon olive oil

1/3 cup Parmesan cheese, plus more for sprinkling

at least 1/3 cup mozzarella cheese (or your favorite cheese—fontina would be nice if the market has it on hand)

salt, to taste

1. Lay the zucchini and squash (Z&S) longways and slice the top $1/3$ off (also longways) and set strips aside.
2. With a small spoon, hollow out the Z&S so that it makes a boat or cup: in this case, a slipper.
3. Set the scooped stuff aside with the strips. Place slippers in baking dish.

FILLING

1. Preheat oven to 375°F.
2. To make the filling, it is easiest to use a food processor, but chopping the ingredients is also fine. Chop or process excess Z&S along with the basil.
3. In a mixing bowl, combine the Z&S/basil mixture, $1/2$ cup bread crumbs, 1 tablespoon olive oil, $1/3$ cup Parmesan, $1/3$ cup mozzarella (or more—more is better), and salt, to taste.
4. Spoon mixture into the slippers, sprinkle more bread crumbs on top of them, cover with foil, and bake for 35 minutes (more or less, depending on your oven).
5. Take out and let stand for a few minutes to set. Then sprinkle with more Parmesan and salt, garnish with fresh basil leaves, and serve.

This is great as a side dish, but, because of the cheese, it can serve as a vegetarian meal all on its own.

Serves 4.

from Tony Senés

THE SCOVILLE TORTILLA

Scoville Unit charms fans with carnival-pop keyboards, sweetly sentimental lyrics, and catchy choruses that bring Buddy Holly to mind—and with a name that refers to the heat measurement of chili peppers, it's obvious that this New York and Connecticut quartet is really into food. Shortly after I first met their keyboardist, Tony Senés (one of my boyfriend's college buddies), we went food shopping together to prepare a Spanish-themed New Year's Eve feast. This Spanish tortilla, a thick egg-and-potato omelet, was the menu highlight. I ought to warn you, though—despite Tony's detailed instructions, this recipe isn't meant for novices. Even accomplished cooks may need to try it a few times before they get the eggs just right. Fortunately, the garlic aioli that goes with the recipe is impossible to ruin, and it's delicious enough to save the dish, even if you burn the tortilla a little. Once you do master it, though, it makes fantastic road food. "It can be served cold but doesn't need to be kept in constant refrigeration," Tony notes, "which makes it a killer tour food for a cooler in the van."

INGREDIENTS:

Wine (for drinking while you cook)

$1/2$ cup olive oil—the more virgin the oil, the better the taste

Two cloves garlic, sliced

10 medium-sized potatoes, peeled and sliced $1/8$-inch thick

Half of an onion, diced

Salt

A dozen eggs

Pepper

Water or milk (optional)

DIRECTIONS:

1. Pour yourself a healthy glass of wine and keep a bottle handy; this recipe takes at least an hour.

2. In a very large skillet over medium heat, pour in the olive oil and let it get good and hot.

3. Add the garlic slices and fry until they are nice and crispy, and then remove. This will flavor the oil nicely.

4. Turn the heat down to low and add the potatoes. Let the potatoes cook for a few minutes before you add the onions.

5. Fry the potatoes and the onions until they become soft and turn a nice light brown, and add a healthy amount of salt to taste. (The key thing about a tasty tortilla is that the flavor is all in the potatoes—so the better the potatoes, the better the tortilla. Let the potatoes cook nice and slow, and try to not stir or turn them too much. That is, let them cook on one side, then try and flip all the potatoes so they can cook on the other.) Turn the potatoes once every 2 minutes or so over a controlled low heat.

6. All right, so now we've got some tasty potatoes but our pan is full of olive oil. Drain all the oil you can from the pan—I like to tilt the pan by resting it on another pan and let the oil drain to one side. Once you have drained the oil, put it aside and save it—we'll use it later.

7. Put the potatoes aside and let them cool. Here come the eggs.

8. In a large bowl, whip the eggs with a fork and add salt and pepper. A little water or milk into the egg batter will fluff up the tortilla nicely, but it is not necessary.

9. After the potatoes have cooled down, add all the potatoes to the egg mixture. Stir it up a bit so that there is a good consistent mix of eggs and potatoes.

10. All right, add a few tablespoons of the drained olive oil back into the pan and heat it on medium high. Add the potato-and-egg mixture and reduce the heat to medium-low. Shake the pan to prevent the tortilla from sticking on the bottom, and start forming edges around the sides of the pan with your spatula.

11. Once the bottom has browned a bit and looks tasty, prepare yourself mentally for the Tortilla Power Flip. Find a plate that is as big as the pan, and place it directly on top of the tortilla. In one smooth motion, flip the pan onto the plate so that the cooked side of the tortilla is now showing. Add a little more oil to the pan and slide the tortilla back into the pan. This might get a little messy, and unless you have sufficiently shaken the pan so that the tortilla did not stick, this is the part where tortillas become scrambled eggs with potatoes.

12. Once you have flipped the tortilla, shake the pan some more and re-form the sides with your spatula. It's most effective to use the back side of the spatula for this. Cook the tortilla on this side, shaking frequently while letting the eggs set. The tortilla is done when you stick a fork in it and nothing comes out.
13. Flip again onto a plate and let it cool for 10 minutes.
14. Slice it up like a pizza or cut into squares and enjoy.

AIOLI-GARLIC MAYO

Tortillas are so killer with this sauce.

INGREDIENTS:

4 cloves garlic, diced or mashed in a garlic press

1 teaspoon salt

1 teaspoon plus 1 tablespoon olive oil, divided

4 tablespoons mayo

DIRECTIONS:

1. Dice the garlic into very small pieces or run it through a garlic press, and pour roughly a teaspoon of salt on the pile.
2. Pour a teaspoon of oil onto the pile as well and then mash everything together with a butter knife.
3. Once it has taken on a smooth consistency, almost like very soft butter, mix it in a small bowl with 4 tablespoons of mayo.
4. Add a tablespoon of olive oil and whip the mixture with a fork until it looks like mayo again.
5. It's ready to go right now, but it might be too garlicky for some. Keep adding mayo and olive oil while stirring to weaken the garlic flavor to taste.

Serves 8–10.

from James Hepler

LIFE OF THE PARTY CHICKEN ON A STICK

Bouncy and noisy Sorry About Dresden was formed by Matt Oberst (vocalist, guitarist, and brother of Conor from Bright Eyes) after he moved from Omaha, Nebraska, to Chapel Hill, North Carolina. Drummer James Hepler is the band cook, and this recipe for chicken skewers—which truly will take your party to the next level—is something he holds dear. "I hate to share this," Hep says. "If I ever go to a party where someone else made it, I'm cracking skulls." If you're a Chapel Hill resident, cook this at your own risk.

INGREDIENTS:

Bamboo skewers

1/2 medium sweet onion cut into a few pieces

4 cloves fresh or 2 teaspoons jarred minced garlic

Lemon zest from one lemon (just the yellow part of the peel, grated)

1 1/2 tablespoons brown sugar

2 tablespoons fresh lemon juice

1/2 cup soy sauce

1 tablespoon + 1 teaspoon curry powder

About 6 boneless, skinless chicken breasts, cut into 1-inch pieces (I buy breast tenders instead of breasts so I don't have to spend half of my time cutting chicken. You can also use pork.)

DIRECTIONS:

1. Submerge the skewers in a bowl or pan of water—they need to soak for at least an hour before you cook the chicken.
2. Combine all of the ingredients except the meat in a blender and blend the shit out of it.
3. Pour the wonderful-smelling marinade over the chicken and marinate for at least 2 hours in the fridge.
4. Slap the chicken onto the skewers and grill them. My God. You will be a hero.

^{1}/$_2$ cup smooth peanut butter

^{1}/$_4$ cup lime juice

^{1}/$_4$ cup water

2 tablespoons soy sauce

1 tablespoon honey

^{1}/$_2$ teaspoon sesame oil

1 clove fresh or ^{1}/$_2$ teaspoon jarred, minced garlic

^{1}/$_2$ teaspoon ground coriander

1. Blend this shit up in your blender.

Serves 10–12.

from Anita and Kevin Robinson

BEST GUACAMOLE EVER

&

HOTT BOILED PEANUTS

Husband-and-wife duo Anita and Kevin Robinson started Viva Voce, which is Italian for "by word of mouth," in their hometown of Muscle Shoals, Alabama, and then relocated to Portland, Oregon, where their shimmering and triumphant sound fits right in with the neighborhood music scene. They offer this pair of his-and-hers recipes—the peanuts are Kevin's and the guacamole is Anita's—which brings up an important tip: When hosting a party with your partner, cook separately, but entertain together. Seriously, tensions run high during the last hours before guests arrive, and nobody wants to argue about who gets to gleefully taste for salt while the other laboriously chops a tear-inducing onion. Rather than collaborate on one painstaking recipe, make two, independently yet lovingly. Trust me—you'll end up with more food and fewer fights every time.

BEST GUACAMOLE EVER

INGREDIENTS:

4 avocados

1 teaspoon fresh lemon juice

1 green onion, chopped

10-ounce can Rotel diced tomatoes with
    chilies (or whatever brand you can find,
    drained)

Salt and fresh-ground black pepper, to
    taste

1/4 cup sour cream

Tortilla chips

DIRECTIONS:

1. Peel, pit, and mash the avocados with the lemon juice and half the chopped onion.
2. Then add the Rotel tomatoes (completely drained) and mix it all together with a little salt and lots of pepper.

3. Garnish with sour cream and the remaining chopped green onion, and serve with tortilla chips.

Makes about 4 cups.

HOTT BOILED PEANUTS

INGREDIENTS:

24-ounce bag o' raw peanuts (in their
shells)
Water
Salt
Two 5-ounce bottles of Tabasco (original
flavor)

6-pack of beer (bottled PBR works best)
Cayenne pepper

EQUIPMENT:

1 deep soup pot & drainer
2 big spoons

DIRECTIONS:

1. Wash raw peanuts thoroughly in cool water; then soak in water for about 30 minutes before cooking.
2. Put peanuts in a deep, heavy soup pot and cover completely with water. Because the shells of some peanuts absorb more salt than others, it's best to begin with 1 tablespoon of salt for each 2 cups of peanuts; you can add more salt to taste later. I prefer them salty as hell, so I usually double this.
2A. Bring water to a boil and add entire 1st bottle of Tabasco with 1/2 a bottle of beer to the water.
2B. Drink rest of beer.
2C. Add a "shot" of cayenne pepper. I usually go for a generous handful, but this is where you can go more or less, to desired spiciness.
3. The cooking time is slightly different for the different varieties of raw peanuts. For instance, the cooking time for a freshly pulled green peanut is shorter than for a bag of packaged raw peanuts. I prefer the bag kind you get at the store, but if you bought them freshly pulled, just keep a closer eye on them.

4. Boil the peanuts for about 35 minutes, then taste one. If they are not salted enough, add more salt. Taste again in 10 minutes, both for saltiness and to see if the peanuts are fully cooked. When fully cooked, the texture of the peanut should be similar to that of a cooked dry pea or bean—soft but not mushy. If they're still not ready, continue tasting every 5 minutes until they have a satisfactory texture. Or check that your stove still works.

5. Drain peanuts after cooking or they will continue to absorb salt and become oversalted. Return peanuts to original soup pot and add 2nd entire bottle of Tabasco. With two large spoons, mix up the peanuts and let sit for about 10 minutes. Taste again for spiciness. If you're feeling brave, you can mix in another small shot of cayenne pepper.

So now you've got 5 more beers to have your boiled peanuts with. Enjoy!

P.S. Boiled peanuts are usually served as a snack, but I've had them as a meal many times. It's best to eat them while they're hot out of the pot, but they also can be served at room temperature, or chilled in the refrigerator and eaten cold, shelling as you eat them. It's best to eat them outside, where you can throw the shells on the lawn—preferably the front yard, where this can also serve as a conversation starter.

Serves 8.

SANDWICHES | **THREE**

ANYONE CAN MAKE a decent sandwich. The ability to layer meat and cheese between slices of bread is practically innate, but I decided to include a chapter on sandwiches anyway because there were so many bands with limited kitchen skills who wanted to share their favorite on-the-road meals. These recipes don't require much culinary prowess or cooking equipment—if you've got a toaster and a frying pan, you can try them all—but they're creative and impressive enough for a special lunch or even dinner.

Plus, since you don't have to invest too much time, money, or energy in a sandwich, this chapter gives non-cooks an opportunity to try out some more adventurous recipes. Death Cab for Cutie's Veggie Sausage and Peanut Butter Sandwich may sound a little gross, but you can whip it up in a couple of minutes and it just might become a favorite on-the-go meal. If that's too much of a leap for you, try an everyday sandwich that's elevated by one inventive ingredient—Hayden takes the club sandwich to a new level by adding a layer of frozen lettuce, and Hudson Bell perfects a simple ham-and-cheese number with an unlikely homemade condiment.

There are plenty of options for vegetarians here, too. Mates of State bring the understated flavors of pear, avocado, and goat cheese together for comforting *panini* sandwiches, and while My Morning Jacket's "You Can Care If You Wanna" Sandwich may seem like much ado over a fake chicken patty, the results are surprisingly delicious. Belle & Sebastian's HRT allows vegetarians to forgo bacon on their BLT without sacrificing the opportunity to indulge in incredibly unhealthy fried food, and the Amphetameanies' promotional Ham-Feta-Beanie, developed as a record-release party snack, can be made meatless, too.

Whether you're planning a picnic or a casual dinner, these are the recipes to try when you don't want to spend your whole day in the kitchen. Dig in.

from Mick Cooke

HAM-FETA-BEANIE

Unless you're a Scottish ska freak, you may not be familiar with Glasgow's long-running, pun-loving, nine-piece ska band, the Amphetameanies, but you'd probably recognize a few of its members. Established in the mid-'90s, the band featured Alex Kapranos on rhythm guitar, until he left the band in 2003 to focus on Franz Ferdinand. Mick Cooke continues to play trumpet for both the 'Meanies and Belle & Sebastian. "We made this sandwich for the launch party for the first Amphetameanies album," he says, "and the name gives away the ingredients."

INGREDIENTS:

Sliced ham from the deli counter (or "cheating ham" for vegetarians)

Feta cheese (or its vegan counterpart), crumbled

Store-bought three-bean salad or canned baked beans

Mayonnaise, to taste

Pita bread

DIRECTIONS:

When we made these sandwiches, we planned to use the three-bean salad you can buy from supermarkets here in Glasgow, but I remember we actually washed the sauce off baked beans to save some money! Then we put some mayo in and served it in pita breads. Very tasty, very nutritious.

Serves 1 or a crowd,
depending on how much you stock up on ingredients.

from Mick Cooke

HRT—HALLOUMI, RADICCHIO, AND TOMATO SANDWICH

Mick Cooke splits not only his horn-blowing skills but also his sandwich-making exper-tise between his two bands, Belle & Sebastian and the Amphetameanies. The retrieval of this recipe involved meeting up with the tireless trumpeter after a Belle & Sebastian show at SXSW in Austin, Texas. Extensive text messaging helped us to find each other above the din of drums and drunkards, but I still got a taste of Mick's Scottish burr through my phone's glowing screen when he wrote, "I am at the sunken bit to the left of the stage but I shall come out front."

Mick explained this recipe in detail over a round of Shiner Bocks. It's something like a BLT, but fried Halloumi cheese stands in for the bacon, and spicy radicchio, in place of bland iceberg lettuce, gives it a kick. You may need to scour your local gourmet grocery store for the Halloumi, but this creamy white cheese is worth the search.

INGREDIENTS:

Halloumi cheese

Whole wheat bread, toasted

Radicchio

Cherry tomatoes, chopped

Mayonnaise, to taste

DIRECTIONS:

1. Basically, all you do is chop the Halloumi cheese into slices about half a centimetre thick, and fry the slices in a frying pan, with no oil, on both sides, until they are nice and brown.
2. Then stick a couple of slices between some nice wholemeal bread, along with the radic-chio (or any kind of lettuce would do just fine) and some chopped tomato (cherry is best).
3. Slap on a bit of mayo and, hey presto, a great veggie alternative to a BLT. It's particu-larly good if you toast the bread first.

Serves 1.

from Chris Mills himself

BOLOGNA, MUSTARD, AND PICKLE SANDWICH

Chris Mills recorded his grandest album, *The Wall to Wall Sessions*, with a 17-piece band (including members of the Sea and Cake and Giant Sand) after only two formal rehearsals. The songs were performed live during the course of two and a half days and recorded and mixed on the spot with a two-track tape machine. This all went down in Chicago—during a blizzard. The results are awe-inspiring. Rock can get complicated, but this sandwich isn't. Feed to those who are living the dream.

"This is one my mom used to make for me all the time. I know it sounds kinda gross but it's actually quite delicious."
—CHRIS MILLS

INGREDIENTS:

2 slices of white bread

French's yellow mustard

2 slices Oscar Mayer Bologna

Sweet pickles

DIRECTIONS:

1. Slather one side of bread with a generous helping of yellow mustard.
2. Layer bologna on top of bread.
3. Slice enough sweet pickles to cover the bologna.
4. Cover the bologna with pickles.
5. Top with second slice of bread.
6. Cut diagonally.

Best served with soda, potato chips, and cartoons.

Makes 1 sandwich.

from Chris Walla

VEGGIE SAUSAGE AND PEANUT BUTTER SANDWICH

The peanut butter sandwich is probably the most frequent meal made in the vans of touring bands, since it only has two ingredients and neither requires refrigeration. When Death Cab for Cutie upgraded from a crowded van to a tour bus equipped with a kitchenette, they raised the bar on their peanut butter sandwich, too. Sitting on the boardwalk at New York's Coney Island, the band raves about their unusual creation.

"One of the staples of my diet is veggie sausages, either links or patties—whichever kind is around—fried up on peanut butter toast," guitarist Chris Walla says. "It sounds dreadful. But it's really not."

"Yeah, it's super good," singer Ben Gibbard adds. "Shouldn't be tasty, but it is."

Even Jason McGerr, the drummer, who has been silent all day, chimes in, "One time we got the curry version of the sausages, and the melted peanut butter became more like a peanut sauce. It was like a delicious Thai sandwich."

When bassist Nick Harmer nods with approval, it's unanimous. You've got to eat it to believe it, but somehow, this protein-packed sandwich really hits the spot.

INGREDIENTS:

Bread	Veggie sausage
Oil	Peanut butter

DIRECTIONS:

1. Put the bread in the toaster.
2. While it's toasting, heat a little bit of oil in a frying pan.
3. Cut up some veggie sausage and throw it in the pan. Move the sausage around with a spatula until the bread is done toasting.
4. Then, spread peanut butter on the warm bread and put the sausage between two slices.

Makes 1 sandwich.

from Hayden himself

EXPLODING SANDWICH

Every couple of years, Toronto-based singer-songwriter Hayden releases a record without much fanfare. He tours infrequently and travels light—it's usually just him, his acoustic guitar, and a pocketful of jokes to drop between songs, but his loyal listeners wait patiently and flock to his shows whenever he comes around. His cult of fans includes Steve Buscemi, who commissioned him to write the title track for his 1996 film, *Trees Lounge*, and still shows up whenever Hayden plays in Brooklyn.

Some of Hayden's songs are hauntingly pretty and pensive; others allude to food. He's been known to sing about ditching work in favor of a big diner breakfast, sharing a pizza in bed, or passing along fortune cookie wisdom to a friend with the blues. If you're a Hayden super-fan, then you already know that seven and a half minutes into the final track on the (now out-of-print) original release of 1995's *Everything I Long For*, a goofy voice with a faux-French accent comes on to guide listeners through the making of a sandwich. The re-release of this record doesn't have the hidden track, so Hayden gave us the okay to publish the recipe.

INGREDIENTS:

Lettuce

Barbecued chicken

Bacon

3 slices of bread

Mayonnaise

DIRECTIONS:

This club sandwich is highly known for its frozen yet explosive moisture crunch. This is achieved through—before the sandwich is made—running lettuce under some water, wrapping it in some paper towels, and placing it in your freezer. Once that's done, you can continue with making your sandwich.

1. Now, you should already have barbecued your chicken, so have that available on your plate at your side. Then, take some bacon, fry it up nice and crispy. *Mm-mm-mm-mm.*

2. Put three slices of bread in the toaster. Toast them. Take them out.

3. So, let's begin. Put down one slice of toast. Follow with sliced chicken, sliced to your preferred thickness. You know, this is your sandwich, after all.

4. Put on the chicken, run to the freezer, and get out your lettuce. Now, hopefully the lettuce won't be frozen to the paper towel, but if it has, then just remove it, and put it on top of the chicken.

5. Then put on some crispy bacon. Did I already?—[*laughs*] This might be the second layer of bacon, but bacon is good for you!

6. And then you mayo-up a piece of toast, put that on top, and then repeat the process for the second layer of chicken and bacon and frozen lettuce.

7. Slice diagonally across the bread twice, and you have a tasty club sandwich with the frozen explosive lettuce because freezing it, you know, you get the water and it's frozen and it explodes when it melts. [*Sigh.*]

Makes 1 sandwich.

from Hudson himself

RIVERBOATS

Baton Rouge–born and San Francisco–based, Hudson Bell's music reaches across the gap from his current home back to his birthplace. You can hear a small drawl in his spare vocals, and warm acoustic guitars are paired with fuzzy electric guitars. This recipe is an ode to the slow, Southern lifestyle of his youth, but it must be the city-dwelling penny-pincher in him who makes half a pound of deli meat last all week. The key to this sandwich is its condiment—the mustard-onion-poppy butter that needs to be made in advance. Try it on turkey or roast beef sandwiches, too, or if you're really broke, spread it on some toast.

INGREDIENTS:

1 stick butter

4 tablespoons mustard (I use Dijon)

2 tablespoons onion powder (not onion salt)

4 tablespoons poppy seeds

12 rolls

1/2 pound ham

1/2 pound Swiss cheese

DIRECTIONS:

1. Melt butter.
2. Add mustard, onion powder, and poppy seeds, and mix well. Allow to set at room temp for 4–6 hours.
3. Spread butter mixture on both sides of a roll. Add ham and Swiss cheese.
4. Wrap in foil and warm in a 350°F oven for 15–30 minutes.

    Man in a rocking chair. "Just as good on both sides of the river," he says, wind blowing, sun blazing down on the stream shifting by. He seems to be enjoying one of what you would make here. He sips some iced tea.

Makes 12 sandwiches,
but you don't have to make them all at once.

from Kori Gardner Hammel

PEAR AND GOAT CHEESE *PANINI*

Just when it seemed impossible for pop duo and married couple Jason and Kori Gardner Hammel to get any cuter, they went ahead and reproduced. At eighteen months old, their adorable daughter, Magnolia, started tagging along on tours. "We're definitely cooking more these days due to the family time it creates," Kori explains. "We aren't vegetarians, but we rarely cook meat for ourselves. Magnolia doesn't like to eat meat—although, if anything is shaped like a ball, she'll shove it down. Recently, when she was exposed to meatballs, all she kept saying was, 'More balls!'" This meatless, mellow, and satisfying sandwich is a staple in the young family's diet. To give it a little kick, try smearing a bit of hot honey mustard on the bread along with the goat cheese.

INGREDIENTS:

Panini bread

2 avocados

salt

goat cheese

2 ripe pears

DIRECTIONS:

1. Toast *panini* bread in oven until crispy.
2. Slice and salt avocado.
3. Spread goat cheese on both sides of *panini* bread.
4. Add sliced pear and avocado.
5. Eat!

Makes 4 panini sandwiches.

from his wife

KERI'S VEGAN GREEK SANDWICHES

With a gravelly voice that sometimes sounds like a dusty echo of Tom Waits, M. Ward digs down deep to the roots of American folk and country—but he's not a Southern blues man. The Portland, Oregon–based singer-songwriter is a big name in indie rock. He's collaborated with Bright Eyes, My Morning Jacket, and Rilo Kiley's Jenny Lewis—he even sang Jeff Lynne's part on Jenny's good-times cover of the Traveling Wilburys' "Handle With Care." Matt's wife, Keri, shares this recipe—which is more of a smorgasbord of sandwich fillings than a straight-up how-to. With so many tasty, vegan-friendly ingredients, you can't go wrong.

INGREDIENTS:

1–2 tablespoons of fresh tahini

1 garlic clove, crushed or put through garlic press

Juice of 1/2–1 lemon

3–4 good handfuls of fresh mixed salad greens

Salt

1 cucumber, diced

About 12 pitted kalamata olives, sliced or whole

About 12 *peperoncini*, sliced

1 teaspoon dried oregano

Fresh ground pepper

A bag of nice flatbread (i.e., pita bread or naan)

Hummus or "baba ghanoush"

EXTRA OPTIONS OR SUBSTITUTIONS:

Garbanzo beans, drained and rinsed

Roasted red peppers

Pickled or raw sliced red onions

Sliced avocado

Toasted sesame seeds

DIRECTIONS:

1. In a small bowl, whisk together tahini, garlic, and lemon (to taste), slowly adding a bit of warm water until the dressing is the consistency you desire. It doesn't take much. Set aside.

2. Place salad greens in a big salad bowl and sprinkle them with a little salt and toss gently.

3. Add the cucumber, kalamatas, *peperoncini*s, and whatever extras or subs you like. Toss again gently.

4. Slowly add the dressing until you've got as much as you like on there. Toss again.

5. Sprinkle the oregano over the leaves and grind on some pepper.

6. Warm up your flatbread in a toaster oven or in a skillet on the stove. Spread a dollop of hummus or baba ghanoush over the bread, then spoon out some salad onto the bread, fold it up, and eat it.

   Tip: If you don't wanna make the tahini dressing, try Karam's tahini garlic sauce.

Serves 2.

from Jim James

THE "YOU CAN CARE IF YOU WANNA" SANDWICH

The first time I saw My Morning Jacket play, they'd just released *At Dawn* on vinyl and were selling copies of it on their merch table at New York's Bowery Ballroom. I already had it on CD, but couldn't resist buying the double LP, despite the fact that it would never fit in my bag and I'd have to hold it for the whole show. As I was shifting it from one arm to the other, I bumped into a long-haired guy with a scraggly beard who broke into a huge smile when he saw the record. It was Jim James, trying to squeeze through the crowded room. "Oh, thank you so much for buying this," he said, hugging me, and patting me on the back, even though we'd never met. "We're so excited to have it on vinyl. I hope you like it!" Minutes later, My Morning Jacket tackled the stage with the one-two punch of Jim's hypnotizing tenor and the band's fierce brand of Southern rock. Several records later, they surge between catchy pop choruses and space-rock jams and continue to turn stiff hipsters into gently swaying hippies—and they still sound better on vinyl.

Jim's singsongy Louisville accent shines through this recipe, and, if you catch the reference, you can almost hear him humming a certain song off Outkast's *The Love Below* as he adds the sour cream.

"i'm a relatively simple eater myself, a good sandwich is always what i make when i'm alone, but we all really love getting together with all our friends and hangin and jammin on some tunes and gettin down and stuff, we tend to do that on the road with peeps and at home. our drummer patrick hallahan is an excellent chef. being a simple cook, one of my fave culinary delights is the 'you can care if you wanna' sandwich."

—JIM JAMES

2 pieces wheat bread (any kind)

1 vegetarian chicken patty (my favorite is
morningstar farm's "chik patties")

a tablespoon or so of sour cream

1 piece farmer cheese (a mild bland
cheese)

1 piece sharp cheddar cheese

2 claussen sweet pickle slices

1. toast da bread to perfection.
2. toast, fry, or zap the chik patty to perfection.
3. spread ("spread-spread for me"—thanks, andre) the sour cream onto the bread.
4. put da cheese on da bread, one on de top, one on de bottom.
5. put da pickles on top of de cheese.
6. put the perfectly toasted chik patty on de pickles.
7. put de other piece of cheese and then bread on top of de chik patty.
8. eat the perfect creation of goodness.

Makes 1 sandwich.

MAIN COURSES FOR CARNIVORES | FOUR

WHEN YOU TELL a die-hard meat-eater that you're collecting recipes from indie rock bands, the first thing they'll ask is, "Aren't they all vegetarians?" But this chapter is a testament to the fact that many band members are proud carnivores—even some of the borderline punk or hippie bands will surprise you with a meaty recipe.

Nowadays, I know lots of self-proclaimed vegetarians who do eat fish, though I've got plenty of other friends (many of whom come from land-locked states) who'll eat anything *but* seafood. Others avoid red meat, but are happy to chow down on fish or chicken. Throw in a handful of food allergies and the epidemic of lactose intolerance, and planning a dinner party menu that accommodates all your guests can be a truly distressing ordeal. I can't help with all your friends' food issues, but this book is set up to accommodate some basic dietary concerns. If you're in the mood for veal, pork loin, wild boar, or venison, you've come to the right place. This chapter also includes plenty of poultry and some carnivorous-lite dishes (like fish tacos from RJD2 and an amazing simple recipe for clam sauce from the Velvet Teen). Grab your boil-in-a bag Salisbury steak, and get started.

from John Navin

PASTA BOLOGNESE

Chicago-based brothers John and Frank Navin of the Aluminum Group make shimmering synth-pop, and they're also avid cooks. Fusing their favorite activities, the duo recently teamed up to present a music-infused cooking class at Chicago's Whole Foods. They prepared a full Italian meal that included this traditional slow-cooked pasta sauce, sautéed spinach, salad, *panna cotta* with fruit compote, and a selection of perfectly paired wines. In this recipe, it may seem strange to simmer the veal in milk, but this decidedly un-kosher step tenderizes the meat for delicious results.

> "okay, so this is one of the finest and most classic pasta sauces in the world!!! you go buy a couple bottles of a good red Tuscan wine, a baguette of crusty Italian bread, whip up this sauce—and, man-oh-man, you can't lose, in fact, you'll instantly charm the pants (or skirt) off the one you're with, seriously!"
>
> —JOHN NAVIN

The
MEAT
Section

INGREDIENTS:

5 tablespoons of unsalted butter

2 tablespoons of finely minced onion

2 tablespoons of finely minced celery

2 tablespoons of finely minced carrots

3/4 pound ground veal

1 cup of organic whole milk

1 cup of dry white wine

One (28-ounce) can of diced tomatoes

1 pound of spaghetti

freshly grated Parmesan cheese

kosher salt

DIRECTIONS:

1. heat the butter in a sauce pan and add the onion, celery, and carrots, and cook for approximately 6 minutes. add the ground veal, and sauté for another 3 minutes.

2. add milk and bring to a simmer, continuing until the milk evaporates and only the clear fat remains.
3. add white wine and repeat simmering process, until the wine has evaporated.
4. add the tomatoes and their juices and simmer at very, very low heat, covered, for 3 hours.
5. this sauce is a rich, delicate and extremely classic sauce from Bologna. the layers of dairy, veal, wine, and vegetables are all there—having slowly come together during the three-hour simmering time of the sauce.
6. cook the sauce gently, stirring occasionally. It's not the quickest sauce, but it is well worth your effort.

"buonissimo! che buono!!" you'll hear your invited guest exclaim, as he (or she) grinds their index finger, back and forth, into their cheek. that's the Italian gesture for showing how good something tastes. that's the gesture you'll see.

when cooking your pasta, reserve about half a cup of the pasta water to add back when you're mixing the Bolognese sauce with the pasta—a little water helps to distribute the sauce evenly. and then sprinkle freshly grated Parmesan and kosher salt and fresh ground pepper to taste. (do not pepper the sauce while cooking, 3 hours of simmering turns pepper bitter!)

buon appetito! con amor, il aluminium gruppo! ciao! baci!

Serves 4.

from Nate Query

PORK LOIN WITH POBLANO CHILIES

When I asked my friend Mike if he wanted to come over for dinner and sample the Decemberists' recipe that I was about to test, he said, "I don't know—does it involve pantaloons?" Sadly, no. But it does involve pork tenderloin! There's nothing fey about this dish from bassist Nate Query. It's hearty and spicy and stands up to his super-strong margarita—don't miss Nate's bonus recipe at the end.

INGREDIENTS:

Mushrooms, 4

Serrano chili, 1

Poblano chilies, 1 or 2

Onion, a half, maybe a whole one

Garlic, 4 cloves or so

Pork tenderloin, $1/4$ pound to $1/2$ pound
    per person

Butter, 2 or 3 tablespoons

Cooking oil

Salt and pepper

Cream, $1/4$ cup

Cilantro

Limes

Corn tortillas

Queso fresco

Margaritas

DIRECTIONS:

1. Dice mushrooms, the chilies, onion, and garlic.

2. Cut the pork into medallions about an inch thick. They should all be about the same size.

3. In hot skillet big enough for all the pork, add a tablespoon of butter, maybe more or maybe some cooking oil.

4. Add some garlic, mushrooms, and chilies, but only about a fourth or less of the total you chopped.

5. Fry for a couple minutes.

6. Add the pork, fry for 10 minutes or so on each side, or until almost done.

7. Remove the pork.
8. Add the rest of the stuff you chopped, add salt and pepper.
9. Cook till translucent and soft, 5–10 minutes.
10. Add ¼ cup cream slowly while stirring to avoid curdling, a little more butter, and put the pork back in the pan to simmer for 10 minutes.
11. Garnish with cilantro and lime wedges, serve with corn tortillas, *queso fresco* . . . and margaritas.

A one-pound tenderloin serves 2–4.

SPEAKING OF MARGARITAS, HERE'S MY MARGARITA RECIPE:

INGREDIENTS

1 part orange liqueur (triple sec or Grand Marnier)

2 parts lime juice
3 parts tequila

Shake with ice. Yum.

A shot and a half of tequila makes one drink.

from Aaron Burtch

BBQ STEAK

The recently disbanded Modesto, California, band Grandaddy was so gentle that even a recipe from their drummer, Aaron Burtch, curves prettily across the page and reads like a poem. Sure, it's a recipe for steak that alludes to barbecued kittens, but that's Grandaddy for you. Back in the day, Aaron designed a bunch of the band's concert posters and album artwork. His outdoorsy drawings feature birds, bunnies, pickup trucks, dancing mice, and peace pipes. Since the breakup, he's gotten into the landscaping business, but is still making art on the side.

hey there.
  i know how to bbq a steak.
  get a steak.
  ribeye.
   porterhouse.
    t-bone.
     something like that.
     put it on a plate.
   put olive oil all over it.
    put pepper all over it.
    put salt all over it.
     light lots of charcoal in your weber.
     like way more than you'd use for everyday
     stuff like hotdogs or kittens.
     sit around until it's hot as shit.
    or instead of sitting around, you can
    prepare a vegetable to eat with the steak.

put the steak on.
leave it there until it's a little burny on the
outside.
flip it and do the same thing as on the
other side.
eat it.

Serving size depends on your steak—
figure about a quarter pound of meat per person.

from Galen Polivka

MIDWESTERN-STYLE BRATWURST

Some of the recipes in this book came to me effortlessly, but I had to work for this one. The cookbook just didn't feel complete without a recipe from the rowdiest and brainiest bar band in New York City, so I sent a bunch of e-mails to their guitarist, Tad Kubler, and I even explained the cookbook to front man Craig Finn while we were waiting on a Porta-Potti line at SXSW. He seemed genuinely interested in contributing, but had to excuse himself when his buzzing cell phone indicated a call from an old friend from Minneapolis, rapper Brother Ali. "When you've got a militant, albino Muslim on the line, you've got to take it!" he explained, before telling me to get in touch with his bass player, Galen Polivka, who happens to work at my favorite bar in Manhattan.

Over the course of this recipe courtship, I dragged many friends to Hi Fi, ordered a few rounds of Maker's and ginger ales, and put a lot of quarters in the jukebox, but as much as he wanted to help, Galen couldn't think of a good recipe. When I finally asked, "Wait, where are you from again? Don't you know how to make beer brats?" his eyes lit up, and I received this incredible essay and parking lot–ready recipe a few days later. I think you'll agree that it was worth my perserverance.

"In my home state of Wisconsin, the culinary art of Bar-B-Q is taken quite seriously, indeed. In Green Bay, at historic Lambeau Field, tens of thousands of inebriates can be found hours before kickoff in the bitter cold, hunched over their Weber grills. In the fairer seasons of spring and summer, in the parking lot of Miller Park, home of my beloved True Blue Brew Crew (that would be the Milwaukee Brewers, to the uninitiated), the sweet smell of mesquite is pungent.

"A conservative estimate would place the probability of bratwurst being prepared over these coals at about 95 percent. It would also be more than safe to say that those gamely and lovingly handling the tongs would be grossly underprepared if not sipping from an ice-cold beer to help them maintain laser-like, surgical focus (GBV reference intentional). Given Wisconsin's large contingent of those of German descent, the enthusiastic overconsumption of said country's two finest exports should surprise no one.

"As for the feast for the ear in such a setting, here is where any continental European influence ends with a deafening, resounding thud. Any blaring of Kraftwerk through car stereo speakers will be met with confused stares at best, and a flurry of fists at worst. The aural equivalent of a beer and a brat is, without question, classic rock.

"That REO Speedwagon '1979 World Series of Rock' T that forty-something-dude is sporting? That Pabst tall boy he's crushing? Go ask him if it's ironic. No, really. Go ask him." —GALEN POLIVKA

INGREDIENTS:

6 cans of domestic beer—in keeping with the Wisconsin theme, Miller High Life, preferably.

2 large onions, roughly chopped

1–2 container(s) sauerkraut—again preferably homemade. Canned will not kill you.

12 bratwursts—if not from a butcher, Milwaukee-made, prepackaged Usinger's or Johnsonville brats will do nicely.

2 sticks of butter

12 hot dog buns or rolls

pickle relish and mustard (optional)

DIRECTIONS:

1. Bring roughly a six-pack of beer to a near boil in a large, deep pot. Place chopped onion, sauerkraut, and brats (poked with a fork, so they do not explode under the influence of heat) into said pot.

2. Simmer lightly, for roughly 2 hours, give or take.

3. About a half hour before you are ready to throw your beer-soaked brats onto your grill, drop in 2 sticks of butter, for an extra savory and artery-hardening flavor delight.

4. Throw now-ready bratwurst onto grill. As they have been soaking for a while in warm beer, they are already fully cooked. Simply grill to taste.

5. Strain the presoaked onion and sauerkraut and add to your brat and bun.

6. Pickle relish and mustard are also delicious with a bratwurst
   Note: Ketchup is a less than acceptable condiment in this case.
7. Eat.

Makes 12 brats.

from John Roderick

ALASKA-STYLE MACARONI SOUP *AL CARNE*

John Roderick, lead man for Seattle's Long Winters, knows that every good cook faces a particular burden: He or she is obliged to share the fruit of his or her labors. This extra-lengthy memoir/recipe offers tips for the selfish chef when faced with hungry siblings and other hangers-on. Cue up some of the Long Winters' dense, orchestral, and subtly catchy pop, and snuggle into a comfy chair for this one—John traces the origins of his Macaroni Soup back to the 1970s, so you'll need some time to savor the story behind it.

"This is a dish that I developed over the course of many years. In the mid-seventies I took an interest in learning to bake cakes, driven by curiosity and the desire to eat the uncooked batter in larger quantities than just 'licking the spoon' allowed. Mom was happy to teach me to bake, partly because those were the early days of feminism and I think she was trying to raise her son to be a sensitive 'cake baker,' and partly because she worked sixty hours a week and this was an activity we could do together. When I turned nine I went to live with my father in Alaska and it was suddenly urgent that I learn to cook properly. The first time he made Kraft Macaroni & Cheese for me after I arrived I watched in horror, perched on a bar stool in his condo kitchen, as he prepared the cheese sauce in a separate pan and then poured it over the macaroni. What was he thinking? What was this madness? The macaroni was the wrong color, the sauce was too runny, and it tasted terrible. I refused to eat it and it caused a big fight. 'Why did you ruin it?' I asked, but he read me the instructions from the back of the box and, astonishingly, he had followed them to the letter. I read them myself, and could make no sense of what I saw, because I had watched my mother make it a thousand times and she had prepared it in only one pot, with a practiced flourish.

"We called down to Seattle once a week to talk to Mom, and once I got her on the phone I quizzed her carefully on how to make Macaroni and Cheese. She said, 'Oh, I never follow the instructions. They tell you to use too much butter. I just take a glob of butter and a splash of milk and that usually does it.' I was troubled by this information, because although Mom's recipe was better tasting and less gross than Dad's, duplicating it would mean using unknowable quantities of the ingredients, deviating from the printed recipe and essentially just wandering off into the wilderness. The only thing I knew how to prepare in the kitchen was cake from a mix, and that involved following the directions to the letter. I could potentially RUIN a whole batch of macaroni if I got the quantities wrong, maybe even poisoning myself or causing an explosion, but a few more plates of Dad's follow-the-recipe slop convinced me that I needed to take the risk.

"The first time I made macaroni I tried to gauge what constituted a 'glob' and a 'splash,' how much salt was in 'a pinch,' and so on, and my instincts proved to be pretty good because the result tasted almost like Mom's own. Dad was glad to wash his hands of the whole thing and from that day forward I was in charge of the Mac and Cheese. Over time I got bolder, mostly as a result of putting too much milk in and discovering that it wasn't so bad that way, until I could make Mac and Cheese with several different types of sauce, from: so thick that the macaroni stood at attention like porcupine quills to: thin like a pasta in au jus. Since I could barely conceive of a diet that didn't include Mac and Cheese at least three times a week (washed down with Tab), and since the other four days a week were taken up with Shakey's Pizza, Wendy's, Rax, and Taco Bell, I saw no reason to learn to cook much else. My various recipes for Mac and Cheese certainly made me something of a celebrity chef amongst my fellow fifth graders.

"Then my little sister came to live with my dad and me. She sampled all the different kinds of Mac and Cheese in my stable during her first month with us and to my surprise declared that her favorite kind was the milky kind, what she called 'macaroni soup,' which had a thin, orange sauce. Thereafter her favorite version was the only version she would eat, and since I was in charge of the Mac and Cheese I was responsible for providing her with the runny kind whenever she called for it. I began to feel somewhat constrained. There were times when I wanted a thicker sauce, but as the older brother, I was duty-bound to uncomplainingly make Macaroni Soup for my sister.

"When we entered our teen years, some of my feelings of brotherly protectiveness wore off. My sister became a belligerent New Waver; she dyed her hair, wore too many belts, and had stupid Punk Rock friends who rode skateboards, had pet rats, and either would never make eye contact or, worse, stared at you with crazy eyes. Still, whenever she heard me in the kitchen she would always come slouching in and hang around, acting like a little girl until I gave her some of my food. This became annoying because she was totally faking that she liked me just so that I would feel like I had a big-brother obligation to cook dinner for her, and it was especially annoying when she insisted that I turn whatever Mac and Cheese I was working on into Macaroni Soup. By this point I had expanded my repertoire to include Chef Boyardee pizza-in-a-box, Swanson's boil-in-a-bag Salisbury steak, frozen Chicken Cordon Bleu with noodles, and my famous spaghetti with Ragú, but Macaroni Soup was my signature.

"Finally, on some occasion where she was smarmily attending my cooking with big doe-eyes, basically taunting me that I was going to have to give her half my macaroni, I hit upon an innovation. Absently looking through the cupboards I spied a small bottle of green food-coloring and surreptitiously put a few drops into the mixture as I made the sauce. I dished up half for her and she recoiled in disgust. 'What's the matter?' I asked, 'Don't you like Punk Rock macaroni? It's got lots of boogers and scabs in it, mmmmm.' I was using reverse psychology. 'Mmmm, it's so good, eat it!' She was grossed out and, even though she knew at some level that I was probably faking, wouldn't eat it. Wow. This was a tremendous discovery. All I had to do was make food look super gross and I wouldn't have to share it with anyone.

"My sister got wise to my tricks pretty fast, so I had to up the ante. The green food-coloring didn't turn her off after the first couple of times, and in fact she started using reverse psychology on ME, saying, 'Oh, it tastes better when it's GREEN, will you please make me some Punk Rock Macaroni Soup?' until my hand was forced. Again searching the cupboards for gross ingredients, I found, in the freezer, a Swanson's boil-in-a-bag Salisbury steak. These Swanson's Salisbury steaks were among my favorite foods, and what could be better than combining it with Mac and Cheese? I boiled it in its bag alongside my boiling macaroni, and at the final stage, I cut open the bag and mixed the Salisbury steak and gravy furiously with the powdered cheese, butter, and milk, creating a meat sauce that was simultaneously orange and gray, with hunks of Salisbury steak throughout. This was too much for my sister. She was beginning to assert her vegetarianism, and my new invention ended forever her freeloading around dinnertime. Shortly thereafter, she discovered Taco Time bean burritos, and their lesser cousins the Taco Bell bean burritos, and she's been living on them ever since.

"I went away to college and lived on dorm food for a year, but then my sophomore year I was kicked out of the dorms and went to live in a decrepit college flophouse I shared with three other guys. There was a Safeway across the street and we usually only bought food we intended to cook immediately, but when you headed out the door to the store it was usually obvious where you were going and if you weren't careful the gang of guys laying around in the living room would get wise and say, 'Hey, would you pick me up some pizza rolls?' or some Jo-Jo's or whatever. Then, when you returned from the store and began cooking your food, you would invariably have two or three people looking to share in your feast as soon as it was done, and in most cases these guys weren't your roommates but were just the Ding-Dongs who hung around the house all day. It was during this period that I recalled the lessons I learned with my sister and perfected the recipe for Alaska-Style Macaroni Soup *al Carne*."

—JOHN RODERICK

FIRST GO TO SAFEWAY AND BUY . . .

INGREDIENTS:

A box of macaroni and cheese, any brand

One package of ramen noodles, any flavor, cheapest

A boil-in-a-bag Salisbury steak, any brand

Large glob of butter, unsalted

Large splash of heavy cream

One can Texas-style chili, no beans

One jalapeño pepper

Optional: one small bottle of green food-coloring

DIRECTIONS:

1. Boil the macaroni until it's almost done, then throw in the ramen noodles, which don't take as long to cook.
2. In a separate pot of boiling water, boil the bag of Salisbury steak.
3. Drain the macaroni and ramen and put in a large glob of butter and a large splash of cream, maybe three glug-glugs.
4. Add the powdered cheese sauce. Throw away the powdered ramen flavoring. Don't put it in the drawer with the ketchup packages because no one is ever going to use it to season anything.
5. Using your finger and thumb, gingerly pull out the Salisbury steak pouch and rip it open with your teeth, pouring the entire contents into the macaroni pot. Run cold water over scalded fingers.
6. Empty the water from that pot and put it back on the red-hot burner, quickly open the can of Texas-style chili and flash-fry it in the bottom of the pot, chopping and adding the jalapeño pepper while the chili fries.

7. Add chili to the macaroni pot. Quickly wash a fork. Stir vigorously, being careful not to let the coagulating ramen noodles wrap around your stirring implement, and chopping up the Salisbury steak so that it mixes with the chili.

8. Depending on the number, voraciousness, and mooching tenacity of Ding-Dongs in the living room, add green food-coloring.

9. Eat directly from pot. Serve with one can of chilled Tab.

Serves ONE!

from El Hefe

EL HEFE'S SPECIALTIES

The following two recipes were lifted directly from an e-mail sent by NOFX's El Hefe. I went ahead and added some loose translations for those who aren't fluent in the language of punk rock. Both dishes are as fast and heavy as NOFX's signature West Coast sound. Turn up *Punk in Drublic* real loud, and chow down.

INGREDIENTS:

1 package of Nissen Top Ramen	1 small can of corn

DIRECTIONS:

"yea, take a pack of top ramen, mix in a can of corn and boil dat shit. yea dat some real ghetto ass gourmet shit."

TRANSLATION:

Prepare ramen according to package directions, adding canned corn to the pot of boiling water along with the noodles. Add seasoning packet as directed. Hooray, it's so cheap yet so yummy.

INGREDIENTS:

1 box of macaroni and cheese	1 can of chili

DIRECTIONS:

"oh yea . . . almost for got. make some mac and cheese, then mix in a can of nelly chilly . . . word. . . . now that's some super fly ass solder in it up shit. . . . no im sayin . . . yea."

Oops, I almost failed to include my other favorite recipe. For this one, prepare macaroni and cheese according to package directions. While the macaroni is boiling, pour the chili into a separate pot and warm over medium heat. Combine the finished macaroni and cheese with the warmed chili. Now, that's delicious! You know what I'm saying? Why, of course you do.

Each recipe serves 1 hungry and broke person.

from Phil's dad, George Sutton

SAUERBRATEN

Rahim is a New York–based band with a catchy and jagged pop sound; Rahim is *not* a trio of mountain men. Still, as drummer Phil Sutton explains below, they know their way around twelve pounds of venison. In hopes of testing this recipe, I e-mailed my friend Steve, the only person I know who hunts and fishes and might have access to the necessary meat. "You're out of luck in the Bambi department," he replied. "The larders are empty. I'm the embodiment of that stupid redneck T-shirt that says *vegetarian* is an ancient Indian word for *bad hunter*." I'll try it with venison next hunting season, but I can attest that the recipe also makes a rich and delicious rump roast—I halved the ingredients to avoid beef overload. Keep in mind that this recipe requires a few days of marinating time, so if you want a to make a Sunday roast, you'll need to start it on Wednesday or Thursday.

"Coming home from tour is a great feeling. No more sleeping on hardwood floors, no more long drives in the smelly van, and no more shitty meals at McDonald's, Burger King, or wherever. Everyone misses home-cooked meals, and Rahim was in need of one desperately. Tour was amazing, but everyone needs to go home.

"Enter my father, George Sutton. A friend of his had gone hunting recently, and brought back copious amounts of venison. And since my dad is the bomb cook, his friend offered up some meat for him to cook up. We were coming home in a few days, so my dad wanted to give us a nice homecoming din-din.

"The recipe below is what he used, and damn, was it good. It feels great to be home after tour, and it feels even greater to have an amazing meal to accompany that." —PHIL SUTTON

10–12 pounds venison (or rump roast)

MARINADE

9 cups water

3 cups balsamic vinegar

10 cloves

2 cloves garlic, crushed or minced

1 large onion

1 cup brown sugar

6 peppercorns

3 bay leaves

DIRECTIONS:

1. Heat above ingredients (except venison) to a boil. Let simmer for 10 minutes.

2. Allow to cool and pour marinade over meat. Marinate for 3–4 days in the fridge.

TO COOK:

2 carrots, chopped

2 celery stalks, chopped

2 onions, chopped

2 bay leaves

1 stick butter

6 cups beef broth

24 gingersnap cookies, crushed

DIRECTIONS:

1. Brown veggies and bay leaves in butter, then add meat and brown.

2. Cover with beef broth and 1 cup marinade. Heat to a rolling boil, then bring down to simmer. (For the sake of food safety, you really need to make sure that the liquid comes to a boil here.)

3. Cover and cook for 1 hour.

4. Add cookies and cook for 1.5 hours at a simmer.

5. To make gravy, pass liquid and veggies through food processor or blender.

   Recommended side dishes: red cabbage and *spaetzle* (a traditional German side dish of tiny egg noodles).

Makes enough to feed a small army.

from Jon Gonnelli's grandfather, Nick Salvemini

PORK CHOPS SALVEMINI

Take a hefty serving of New Jersey hardcore, spoon in some Led Zeppelin swagger, spike it with a shot of AC/DC dynamism, and you've got a little taste of Rye Coalition. On stage, guitarist Jon Gonnelli might kick ferociously, or take off his shoes and dance with every girl who comes within arm's length, depending on his mood. He's even more of a charmer in the kitchen, and his fellow band members rave about his cooking. This recipe comes from Jon's grandfather, who passed away last year. As you're polishing off the requisite bottle of brandy, raise a glass in his honor.

"Here's a recipe taught to me by my grandfather Nick Salvemini. The best part of making this is taking the bread that you bought and dipping it in the juice throughout the entire process. Make sure you dip the bread."

—JON GONNELLI

INGREDIENTS:

12-ounce Jar of *peperoncini* Peppers

4–5 Cloves Garlic (Depending on How Much You Like Garlic)

Olive Oil

2–3 Pork Chops (Prefereably Thick Cut w/ Bone In)

$^1/_2$ Pint of Brandy (A Little Airplane Shot Would Also Do)

1 Loaf of Hard Italian Bread or French Bread

1. Without draining the liquid from the jar, take out about 8 *peperoncini*s, cut off the stems, slice into quarters or halves, and scrape out the seeds. Put on the side. Don't put the jar away yet because you'll use the juice in the jar later.

2. Chop the 4–5 cloves of garlic, the finer the better. Sauté in a large frying pan with a generous amount of oil, enough so that all of the garlic is completely covered. Use a low flame so things don't heat up too fast.

3. Don't Burn the Garlic!

4. Add Pork Chops to garlic and oil. Sear the Pork Chops on both sides. Just let one side turn white and then flip it. You don't want to cook them too much until you add the *peperoncini* juices for maximum flavor. When both sides are seared, turn back to the side you began on.

5. Add quartered *peperoncini*s over pork chops. Also, pour a healthy swig of the *peperoncini* juice in there. I never measure it. I just go with my gut. You definitely don't want to drown the chops, but you want enough in there so that the juices wind up cooking the chops. It usually turns out to be about half the juice in the jar.

6. Finally, throw a shot of brandy in there. And if you have any brandy left over, drink it while the pork chops are cooking. This helps when you need to sit down and eat.

7. When everything is in there, cover the chops and let the steam do its magic. Make sure you flip the chops at some point—inch-thick pork chops need to be cooked for 4–5 minutes per side. Thinner chops require less cooking time. Check the middle of the chop to determine when it's done being cooked. When there's no more pink, you're good to go. Try not to overcook them though. This recipe really lets the tenderness of the chop shine.

Serves 2–3.

from Brian Ritchie

WILD BOAR *RAGÙ*

If adolescence had an official soundtrack, it would be provided by the Violent Femmes. They're not quite indie rock, but if you haven't got their self-titled debut CD in your neatly alphabetized record collection, nestled somewhere between the Velvet Teen and Weezer, then your roommate must have stolen it. Brian Ritchie's acoustic bass line has no doubt rocked your teenage dance parties, and now he's going to up the ante at your next dinner soiree. "My strategy is to eat food at a restaurant and then try to guess how they made it. Then I add my own ideas," Brian explains. "I used to live in Italy, and this is my version of something I had in Florence. This recipe is as good as what you'd get there."

I picked up some wild boar from New York's Citarella Fine Foods, but I had to place an order a few days in advance, and the smallest amount they would sell me was a whopping five pounds of meat. Fortunately, this deeply flavorful stew is something I'll be happy to make again (half the boar is still in my freezer)—but if you don't have easy access to wild boar, try another type of meat, as Brian suggests below.

"*Ragù* is a winter dish characterized by meat and tomatoes. It is traditional to cook it all day, adding more liquid if it starts to dry out. Italians use fresh tomatoes in the summer and canned in winter.

"Making a *ragù* is like playing jazz. You have to be creative, tasteful, and able to adapt to the circumstances. The beauty of ragù is that everybody is free to develop their own. Aside from meat and tomatoes, you can basically add whichever other spices and ingredients appeal to you. If you don't want wild boar, substitute any other meat you like—lamb, pork, veal, beef, or venison. I have made this dish with all of those depending on availability and what looks good at the butcher.

"Note: I do not use a recipe or exact quantities when I cook. These quantities are just to give you a rough idea. Adjust to your own taste."

—BRIAN RITCHIE

1 large Spanish onion (chopped)

2 tablespoons olive oil

2 pounds boneless wild boar meat (cut for stew)

1 can chopped tomatoes

3 bay leaves

1 cup red wine

5 cloves garlic, crushed

3 dried chili peppers (crushed)

1 cinnamon stick

5 cloves

3 sun-dried tomatoes

3 anchovies or 1 teaspoon anchovy paste

Fresh or dried oregano, basil, and sage

1 tablespoon red wine vinegar

Salt and black pepper to taste

Pasta (*pappardelle* or fettuccine)

Grated pecorino cheese (*Parmigiano* is an acceptable substitute, but pecorino, being sheep cheese, complements game)

DIRECTIONS:

1. In a large cast-iron pot, sauté the onion in olive oil until translucent.
2. Add the boar meat and brown. (That is, cook the meat over high heat, turning frequently, just until it's cooked on the outside.)
3. Add the canned tomatoes and the bay leaves.
4. Add the wine.
5. Gradually add the garlic, dried chili, cinnamon stick, cloves, sun-dried tomatoes, anchovies (or anchovy paste), oregano, basil, sage, red wine vinegar, and salt and black pepper to taste.
6. Simmer on low on the stovetop with the lid of the pot slightly ajar, and stir occasionally for at least two hours—or longer if possible. The longer you simmer this, the more tender the meat will become. The ragù is ready to eat when the meat has totally fallen apart and most of the liquid has been absorbed by the meat. Take out the cinnamon stick and bay leaves before serving.
7. Serve over the pasta and top with grated cheese. Accompany with some crusty peasant bread and a good red wine, preferably a strong Italian, like Amarone or Barolo.
   Mangia!

Serves 4 to 6.

from Cale Parks

FRIED CHICKEN WITH BISCUITS AND GRAVY

When I first met Aloha, they were still dragging a vibraphone around the country, and Cale Parks and I weren't old enough to get into bars—the night we met, they were playing a coffee shop. Cale was already an intuitive jazz drummer, though, hitting off-time beats that I couldn't begin to get my head around, and I was just breaking in my mini tape recorder. They were the first band I ever interviewed, and though I had hoped to hear about the romance and adventure of being on tour, they complained of hunger pains. If you feel like feeding them next time they're in town, this fried chicken recipe will make Cale and TJ happy, but make sure you have some meatless side dishes—Tony and Matthew are vegetarians. Buy regular, bone-in chicken pieces—the boneless, skinless variety won't produce enough grease for the gravy, which will be much easier to make if you get a live tutorial from Cale.

The **POULTRY** *Section*

FOR THE CHICKEN, YOU'LL NEED:

1 egg
buttermilk
flour

chicken pieces
olive oil or butter

CHICKEN PREPARATION IS LIKE THIS:

1. mix 1 egg and 1 cup of buttermilk in a bowl.
2. in a separate bowl, measure 1 cup of flour.
3. dip chicken pieces in bowl with wet mix (egg & buttermilk), covering all the chicken with the mix.
4. dip the chicken pieces in bowl with flour, covering the pieces entirely.
5. fry in a skillet with about a tablespoon of olive oil or butter to keep chicken from sticking, until golden and crispy. (make sure the chicken is thoroughly cooked and save the grease!)

Olive oil

Flour

Buttermilk

Frozen biscuits

Grease from fried chicken

BISCUITS* & GRAVY PREPARATION IS LIKE THIS:

1. heat oven to whatever temperature the instructions on the bag of frozen biscuits says, and cook them accordingly.

2. now for the gravy, keep about 2 tablespoons of grease from your fried chicken in the skillet.

3. in the same skillet, mix in about 3 tablespoons of flour and stir it up with the grease.

4. continue simmering and stirring over light heat until it's toasty and nutty looking.

5. then mix in buttermilk until desired consistency‡ is reached (you want it to be kinda thick, but not too thick), and pour over biscuits and enjoy!

Serves 4.

*some might think i'm taking the easy way out, but i usually just use frozen biscuits, they're better than canned, but not as good as from scratch. sorry!

‡getting the right consistency in your gravy is key. it takes a couple of tries unless you're a natural!

from the Oktopus's girlfriend, Alexandra

SPICY *ARROZ CON POLLO*

Dälek packs midsized rock clubs in the US, but thanks to the booming avant-garde music scene overseas, they play to packed arenas in Europe. Some say it's their otherworldly brand of hip-hop that draws the Euro-crowds; others blame it on their umlaut. In any case, the heavily tattooed Oktopus may look awfully tough as he rocks his laptop on stage, but friends know him as Alap Momin, a really nice guy with a top-of-the-line recording studio—which recently relocated from his very accommodating mom's garage to a 1,000-square-foot studio space in Union City, NJ. He doesn't do much cooking himself, but this spicy and hearty chicken recipe is a favorite of his from his favorite girl, Alexandra.

INGREDIENTS:

Approximately 2 pounds chicken thighs

2 garlic cloves

2 Jamaican hot peppers (these are small, red, irregularly shaped hot peppers—Scotch bonnet peppers or habaneros work well, too)

Olive oil

Adobo seasoning

1 small onion

1/2 green or yellow pepper

1 cup wine or beer

2 cups white rice

2 packets Sazón (from the Latin foods aisle)

approximately 3/4 cup chopped cilantro

1 box of frozen peas

1 can of pimentos

EQUIPMENT:

Deep, large skillet or pot

DIRECTIONS:

1. Cut fat from chicken thighs. Chop garlic cloves and Jamaican hot peppers. Use 1 hot pepper for medium spicy or 2 for very spicy.

2. Marinate chicken in olive oil, adobo, hot peppers, and garlic for at least 30 minutes.

3. Meanwhile, chop onion and green or yellow pepper. Sauté for a few minutes. Add marinated chicken thighs, and brown lightly on each side.

4. Add 1 cup wine or beer, 1 cup water, and chopped cilantro. Bring to boil, then lower heat to medium and cook for 20 minutes.

5. After 20 minutes, add 2¹/₂ cups water, 2 cups white rice, and 2 packets of Sazón. Bring to boil, cover, then cook on low heat for 20 minutes, or until water is evaporated.

6. Add frozen peas and pimentos about 5 minutes before water is evaporated. Let sit for 10 minutes before serving.

Serves approximately 6.

from Drew himself

CHICKEN IN COCONUT CURRY

Drew Isleib, whose introspective folk-rock songs generally center around present, past, and future girlfriends (and sometimes the New York subway system), is the king of the couch circuit. For many singer-songwriters, booking a solo tour means setting dates at small clubs and coffee shops across the country—and then trying to find fans or friends in each city who'll lend a couch to sleep on after the show. Drew cuts straight to step two—he just looks for a fan, relative, friend-of-friend, or sociable stranger in each town and offers to play a show in their living room if they'll invite some people over to see the set and let him spend the night. For a shy performer, this would be awkward, but it's hard to faze a natural chatterbox like Drew. Next time his couch tour comes through your house, ask him to come early and make dinner—Drew's creamy, Thai-style curry is perfect for his lactose-intolerant, legume-allergic brethren because it's free of peanuts and milk.

INGREDIENTS:

1 tablespoon of cumin powder, or to taste

10-ounce boneless, skinless chicken breast

10.75-ounce can of condensed tomato soup

14-ounce can of unsweetened coconut milk (Thai Kitchen has a good one, but Goya is not so good. If you accidentally buy a sweetened one, make piña coladas instead.)

a pinch of salt (preferably iodized; it prevents goiters)

a few shakes of pepper

DIRECTIONS:

1. Fill a medium saucepan with enough water to cover your chicken, add about $^1/_2$ tablespoon of cumin, and bring to a boil.

2. Cut chicken breast into strips and add to water.

3. In a separate saucepan over low heat, mix the condensed soup and coconut milk.

4. Add salt, pepper, and another $1/2$ tablespoon cumin, or more to taste.

5. When chicken is white all the way through, transfer it into the tomato and coconut pan.

6. Let simmer, while stirring for 15–20 minutes. Serve in bowls, and for a heartier meal, add a scoop of white rice to each serving.

Serves 2 as a meal or 4 as a first course.

from Chris Saligoe

BRANDY PEACH SAUCE FOR CHICKEN OR TOFU

Chris Saligoe (known to friends as "Sal") splits his time between rocking the bass for Bloomington, Indiana's hardcore heavyweights Racebannon, playing guitar for loopy local band Rapider Than Horsepower, and working as a chef at a health food market called Bloomingfoods. Like most chefs, he's used to cooking in bulk. This really makes a ton of food, so you'll need to scale it down if you're not expecting a crowd.

The peach sauce is 100 percent vegan and Sal also likes it on tofu, but compared to the poultry version, the presentation isn't as nice. My roommate, Steph, who definitely isn't adverse to soy products, was pretty freaked out by the gelatinous look of the peachy sauce over baked tofu. It did sort of resemble a Jell-O mold. Full-flavored free-range chicken breasts also work better than tofu in terms of balancing the sweetness of the sauce, but hey, if you're vegan, you gotta do what you gotta do.

"i wrote this basic recipe while on a smoke break at work, trying to get back on my boss's good side. i had been late to work that morning due to playing a racebannon show the night before. anyhow, peaches were in season, and my boss, christie, loves 'em. the way our rotating menu works, we have a different style or region of cuisine each day, so we've been able to play around with different flavor combinations and cooking methods from all over the world. that day was 'american (comfort food)' day, and those ingredients seemed to fit together. christie liked the recipe, and she got over my tardiness. we're good pals, and we like peaches. still can't play peaches on the stereo, though."

—CHRIS SALIGOE

5 pounds boneless chicken breasts, or 5
    packages of firm tofu

3 medium/large red bell peppers

2 cups orange juice

1 cup olive oil

5 peaches (or 3 cans if you're desperate,
    but this won't taste as good)

3/4 cup brandy

1 tablespoon cinnamon

1 cup brown sugar (or a little more)

1 bunch green onions

salt and pepper to taste

*Note: if you're making tofu, you'll also
    need 1 cup tamari and 1 cup water,
    mixed.*

1. for tofu, slice it how you like, then pour the tamari/water mixture over it and bake for 20–30 minutes at 350°F. make the rest of the stuff when that's in the oven.

2. using a cuisinart/immersion blender/regular blender, puree the red bell peppers, oj, olive oil, 3 of the peaches, brandy, cinnamon, and 1/2 cup of the brown sugar.

3. if you're making chicken, use the sauce to marinate the chicken before you bake it. if you're making tofu, once the initial baking is done, pour off the excess water/tamari mixture and then pour the sauce over the tofu.

4. put the chicken or tofu in a few baking pans without overlapping too much, and sprinkle salt, pepper, and the rest of the brown sugar over the whole thing. slice the rest of the peaches and throw them on top.

5. for tofu, bake in a 350°F oven for 10–15 minutes, or until bubbly and browning. cook chicken breast in 350°F oven for 15–20 minutes (to see if it's done, pierce the biggest, thickest piece and make sure it's not pink inside). garnish with thinly julienned green onions.

6. serve over brown rice.

Serves 15–20.

from Rachel Goswell

CHICKEN FILO PESTO PARCEL WITH PUY PUY

Before Rachel Goswell put out a solo album or was a member of Mojave 3, she got her start as the singer for the UK's Slowdive, one of the defining bands of the early '90s shoegaze scene. Fuzzed-out, wall-of-sound guitar parts are no longer in Rachel's repertoire, but these homey recipes definitely are. The Pesto Parcel is like a Mediterranean-flavored potpie, and the Puy Puy makes an elegant North African–inspired side dish. If you have trouble finding puy lentils, any lentils will do.

CHICKEN FILO PESTO PARCEL

"I made this recipe up the last time I got home from tour. I enjoy making things (relatively) from scratch after time away, it feels nice to settle back into home-cooked food." —RACHEL GOSWELL

INGREDIENTS:

6 sheets of filo pastry (ready-made)

2 boneless, skinless chicken breasts, chopped into 1-inch pieces

a generous amount of extra-virgin olive oil

2 shallots, chopped

1 red pepper, chopped

1 medium courgette (zucchini), sliced

a handful of cherry tomatoes, halved

2 garlic cloves

a slosh of white wine

2 tablespoons of pesto sauce

salt and pepper

DIRECTIONS:

1. Preheat oven to 350° F.

2. If you're using frozen filo dough, take it out of the freezer so it starts to soften.

3. Chop up the chicken breasts into bite-size pieces and fry in a little olive oil for 5 minutes.

4. Throw shallots, pepper, courgette (zucchini), cherry tomatoes, and garlic into a separate pan with a tablespoon or two of olive oil, cook for about 5 minutes on a medium heat until shallots are clear, throw in a slosh of white wine, and simmer until liquid has reduced.

5. Stir in pesto sauce, chicken, salt & pepper (as desired).

6. Grease a casserole dish with some more olive oil and layer the sheets of filo pastry till dish is covered and ends of the filo sheets hang off the sides. Spoon in the chicken mixture, then fold over the filo to make a parcel.

7. Chuck in the oven for approximately 35 minutes, until the filo is crispy and cooked through.

8. Serve with an herby salad and some fries, not forgetting to drink the remainder of the bottle of wine!

PUY PUY

"This is based on a recipe that my dad introduced me to a couple of summers ago. It's full of 'good fat' and to me (and if you like lentils), it's quite 'Moorish.' Something I make up and tend to snack on!! A nice addition is fresh avocado—though this has to be chopped up and thrown in at time of eating as it doesn't keep so well mixed up."

—RACHEL GOSWELL

INGREDEINTS:

Cook up some puy lentils—2/3 cup (follow instructions on the pack!).

Chop up some sun dried tomatoes / alternatively roast some cherry tomatoes.

Chop up some shallots / alternatively a red onion.

Crumble some goat cheese / feta / mozzarella (whichever you prefer!).

DIRECTIONS:

1. Mix it all up in a bowl, then drizzle in a mix of extra-virgin olive oil and red wine vinegar.

2. Season with salt and pepper (as preferred) and throw in some chopped garlic (as desired). This will keep in the fridge in an airtight container for up to 5 days. A perfect companion for bar-b-cues/salads—whatever you fancy!

Serves 4.

from Jake Kiley

ROCK 'N' RAMEN

Southern California's punk rock five-piece Strung Out has been putting out records steadily since 1992. Here, guitarist and budget-conscious gourmand Jake Kiley presents one of the recipes that sustained him over the years. He calls it his "Cordon Bleu–approved Top Ramen," and while that might be a bit of a stretch, it's definitely a treat for those who've been surviving on plain old unseasoned ramen. Plus, it's the most cost-efficient recipe in the entire cookbook. You can get a couple of bags of ramen for a lean fifty cents total, and assuming you have a decently well-stocked kitchen (or know someone who will let you use theirs), you probably have the other ingredients on hand.

INGREDEINTS:

1 package of Creamy Chicken Ramen
1 package of Roast Chicken Ramen
Tabasco sauce
Butter

Pepper
Garlic powder
Parmesan cheese
1/4 cup milk

DIRECTIONS:

1. Ok, first off, I always mix two packs together. Just one ramen is never enough, and part of the key here is mixing flavors. The mix I've found to work best is equal parts Creamy Chicken and Roast Chicken. These flavors blend nicely and don't clash with other seasonings.

2. After boiling the ramen for the normal 2–3 minutes I drain all the water and add in the 2 packs said seasoning. At this point I add 2 splashes of Tabasco, butter, pepper, garlic powder, and Parmesan cheese. How much of these ingredients you add is at your own discretion, but I put in a lot!!

3. Mix it up and you will notice it becomes a very dry, clingy clump of ramen. That's where I add in about a 1/4 cup of milk to give this ramen its creamy, exotic texture. Enjoy!!

Serves 1–2.

from Geoff Abell

SWEET POTATO–MANGO–CHICKEN QUESADILLAS

As guitarist for the Chapel Hill punk band Capsize 7, Geoff Abell spent much of the '90s touring the country. Nowadays, he splits his time fronting the more subdued, lowercase-on-purpose pop trio, tommygun, finishing medical school, and hanging out in the kitchen. There's a lot going on in this quesadilla, so if you want to cut out the chicken and go vegetarian with it, you'll still end up with a flavorful and filling meal. Crack open a cold Tecate, add some lime, and get to work.

"All measurements are approximations, so please tweak this recipe to your liking—just don't burn the tortillas because it really ruins the taste. This is also good in burrito form."
—GEOFF ABELL

INGREDIENTS:

1 large sweet potato diced into 1/2-inch cubes

olive oil

1/2 teaspoon cumin powder plus 1–2 teaspoons more

1/2 teaspoon chili powder

salt, to taste

1 small onion, diced finely

2 large tomatoes, diced

1 mango, diced

fresh cilantro

1/2 hot jalapeño pepper, finely chopped

1 lime

1/2 cup sour cream

1/2 cup goat cheese

3/4 pound–1 pound boneless, skinless chicken breasts cut into strips or small chunks

pepper, to taste

4 large flour tortillas

2 cups grated Monterey Jack cheese

1 avocado

1. Cook sweet potato cubes covered over medium-high heat in a pan with 1–2 tablespoons olive oil until lightly browned and soft inside (about 5–7 minutes). While cooking, stir occasionally, and sprinkle in some ($^1/_2$ teaspoon or so) cumin and chili powder. Salt to taste.

2. Mix onion, tomatoes, mango, cilantro, and jalapeño in a bowl. Squeeze 1–2 teaspoons fresh lime juice into mixture, and save the rest of your lime for the chicken. Set this mango *pico de gallo* aside.

3. Mix sour cream and goat cheese in a bowl and set aside.

4. Lightly brown the chicken on medium-high heat in 1–2 tablespoons olive oil. Add approximately 1–2 teaspoons of cumin and salt and pepper to taste. Squeeze in 1–2 teaspoons of fresh lime juice.

5. Place flour tortilla brushed with olive oil in preheated skillet on medium heat. Spread layer of Monterey Jack cheese (use about $^1/_2$ a cup), then add half the potatoes, half the chicken, a little *pico de gallo*, and then another layer of cheese. Add top tortilla, press down firmly, brush top tortilla with oil, then flip quesadilla when lightly browned.

6. Cook until lightly browned on the other side and inside cheese is melted, and remove from heat. Repeat for the second quesadilla.

7. Add *pico de gallo* and goat cheese/sour cream mixture on top of each quesadilla. Garnish with sliced avocado. Eat.

Makes 2 quesadillas.

from Peter Bauer

FOREIGN CHICKEN DINNER

Every few weeks I encounter a New Favorite Song, and, much like a new puppy or a really cute new pair of shoes, I want to be near my New Favorite Song at all times. Some of these songs aren't actually new (they range from Prince's "Kiss" to Dandy Livingston's cover of Donovan's "There Is a Mountain"), but when I dub them my New Favorite, I listen to them obsessively. (You can find them all by sorting my iTunes by "Play Count.") I've listened to the Walkmen's "The Rat" ninety-two times, and the first time I heard the unmistakable strain of Hamilton Leithauser's voice on "Louisiana," I had to listen to it eleven times in a row. Basically, if the Walkmen were an illegal substance, I'd be in jail. Anyway, Peter Bauer played bass on the Walkmen's first two records, but just to keep things interesting, he switched to organs, piano, and lap steel for their 2006 release, *A Hundred Miles Off*. His recipe doesn't refer to a particular ethnicity, but instead mixes up a bunch of "foreign" ingredients—sushi rice, Thai peanut sauce, Grey Poupon—for a dinner that's decidedly American.

> "Tonight you'll be making a teriyaki style chicken with mushrooms, avocodoes, and sticky rice. As a side dish or antipasto (your choice), you'll be having hot asparagus in a zesty mustard sauce. This is my old lady's favorite meal and I hope you enjoy it, too. Let's get going because you have a lot of chopping to do."
>
> —PETER BAUER

ENTRÉE

INGREDEINTS:

- 1 cup of sushi rice
- 1 container of Mr. Mushrooms (that is, an 8-ounce can of whole button mushrooms, drained, or a small package of fresh mushrooms, stems removed)

1 fresh lemon

2 boneless/skinless chicken breasts

1 avocado

1/2 tablespoon Kikkoman Soy Sauce

2 tablespoons butter

1 tablespoon garlic wok oil (or olive oil
with a clove of garlic pressed into it)

Kikkoman Teriyaki Sauce (lots—at least
1/3 cup)

1 tablespoon Sharwood's Teriyaki with
Black Pepper Sauce

1/2 tablespoon Thai peanut sauce (a small
amount of peanut butter works, too)

salt and pepper to taste

basil (little)

red pepper flakes or cayenne pepper

SIDE DISH/ANTIPASTO

INGREDIENTS:

1 bunch of asparagus

half an 8-ounce jar of Grey Poupon
mustard (1/8 cup)

1/4 cup olive oil

1 tablespoon red wine vinegar

salt and black pepper to taste

dried basil (little)

dried oregano (lots)

DIRECTIONS:

1. Prepare sushi rice according to package directions.

2. Meanwhile, rinse and dice mushrooms, and then set them aside.

3. Rinse asparagus and chop off the tough ends of the stems. Pour water into a pan until the bottom is just covered, and place the asparagus in the pan.

4. Slice lemon into 6 wedges and put aside.

5. Cut chicken breasts into nice, even pieces, trimming away any fat that you see, and set aside.

6. Cut avocado into neat, even slices and peel them.

7. Add soy sauce and butter to a clean pan over medium-high heat. As soon as the butter melts, add the chicken. The chicken will take about five to seven minutes to cook through.

8. While the chicken cooks, add all garlic oil, teriyaki sauces, and peanut sauce, salt, black pepper, basil, red pepper, and the juice of 2 lemon wedges. When the chicken is almost cooked through, add the mushrooms.

9. Steam asparagus for 5 minutes. Meanwhile, mix together the mustard, oil, vinegar, salt, pepper, and herbs—throw in a pinch of basil and a heaping teaspoon of oregano. Drizzle this vinaigrette over the asparagus.

10. Serve the chicken and mushrooms over the rice. For an impressive and professional look, circle the food with avocado slices and remaining lemon wedges. Serve with Dr Pepper or your drink of choice.

Serves 2.

from Dan Matz

SPICY WINGS À LA CHICKIE

In compiling these recipes, I've often found parallels between a band's sound and their cooking style, but that's not the case with Windsor for the Derby. Their mild-mannered music will slowly lure you in, but these fiercely spicy hot wings will hit you like a brick (in a good way). Keep in mind that these aren't Buffalo wings, but I think they're a lot better. They're a natural shade of brown and pack some complexly flavored heat—they're neither artificially orange nor tangy. If you don't have a really sharp knife, or if the idea of cutting through the joints of twelve chicken wings makes you gag, be sure to use pre-cut wings.

INGREDIENTS:

6 tablespoons Louisiana Hot Sauce

4 tablespoons olive oil

4 tablespoons cajun seasoning mix

$1/2$ teaspoon chipotle pepper in adobo sauce, or to taste

2 teaspoons onion powder

1 teaspoon garlic powder

1 teaspoon Dill Weed

1 teaspoon Salt

1 teaspoon Black Pepper

12 Chicken Wings (about 2 pounds), tips removed, then cut into 2 pieces each

DIRECTIONS:

1. Preheat oven to 375°F.
2. Mix all ingredients except wings. Adjust seasoning using the chipotle sauce to your preference. Add wings, toss, and marinate overnight.
3. For extra sauce, blend $1/2$ the above recipe and set aside. This is great for basting or dipping.
4. Line roasting pan or cookie sheet(s) with nonstick aluminum foil.
5. Place wings in pan, do not crowd (about 24 pieces per standard cookie sheet).

6. Roast for 25 minutes, remove from oven, turn and return to oven for another 25 minutes. Remove from oven and pour off fat.

7. Cover loosely with foil, and set aside while you preheat the broiler.

8. When the broiler is fired up, remove the foil. Watching closely, broil wings in pans from the oven 6 inches from broiler on one side until the wings are crisp but not burned, about 1–3 minutes.

9. Serve immediately with ice-cold blue cheese dressing and celery.

Serves 2.

from Will Johnson and Clare Surgeson

SOUTH SAN GABRIEL SWEET POTATOES AND SALMON

Like the San Gabriel River that flows through Central Texas, Will Johnson's well of song-writing inspiration doesn't seem like it'll be running dry anytime soon. The ever-prolific lead man needs a stable of songwriting outlets to manage all his tunes. His rock songs make their way onto Centro-matic records, the more mellow ones work their way into South San Gabriel set lists, and if there's any overflow (and, of course, there is), he records solo. In a world where many bands only give their fans a taste of new music every year or two, Will Johnson offers his a never-ending feast—which brings us to his recipe. "Steamed fresh green beans are a nice complement to this dish," Will says. "We actually eat it too often," his girlfriend and co-contributor Clare Surgeson adds, with a laugh. "I think we're gonna need to buy some new pants."

The
FISH
Section

THE SWEET POTATO PART

INGREDIENTS:

2 medium-sized sweet potatoes, peeled

1 tablespoon butter

$1/4$ cup brown sugar

$1/2$ tablespoon cinnamon

$1/2$ teaspoon nutmeg

$1/4$ cup crushed pecans

$1/2$ cup milk (or more, depending on how
fluffy you like them)

DIRECTIONS:

1. Cut sweet potatoes into approximately 1-inch chunks. Put in a pan and just barely cover with water. Boil until super tender—about 15–20 minutes. They should easily break apart with a fork.

2. Strain and mash up. Throw in the butter, brown sugar, cinnamon, nutmeg, and pecans, and mash at least until the butter is melted.

3. Add milk and mash to desired fluffiness.

INGREDIENTS:

2 tablespoons butter

3/4 pound to 1 pound of Atlantic salmon fillet

DIRECTIONS:

1. Preheat oven to 475°F.
2. Melt butter in glass baking dish.
3. Place salmon skin-side up (or facedown—however you prefer to look at it) in oven-safe dish. Bake for 5 minutes.
4. Remove from oven and flip the salmon over. Bake for another 5 minutes, or until it reaches your desired level of doneness. This will vary according to the thickness of the fillet, but a little of the raw pink inside is fine.
5. Serve. Enjoy. And make some space on that couch for later.

Serves 2.

from Eric Bachmann

SEARED TUNA WITH WASABI-COCONUT SAUCE AND ROASTED-PEPPER RICE PILAF

When I think back to some of the happiest times of my life, I can hear Eric Bachmann's music playing in the background. His old band, Archers of Loaf, was the car stereo soundtrack to many nights of sipping Slurpees with my best friends in high school. When Archers disbanded, Eric started Crooked Fingers—named for his grandfather's CB handle—and my boyfriend, Pete, played me their first record on our first date. On our first vacation together, we found that our North Carolinian pals were also big Archers of Loaf fans and had actually been to their last show ever. In the dark, junkyard-like backyard of their crappy local bar, they broke out into an a cappella version of "Web in Front," which remains the most joyful, punk rock thing I've ever heard. In that moment, I felt so lucky that my life was happening to me.

But, because I'm a bit of a pessimist, I really hoped I'd never meet Eric Bachmann. I feared that no mortal man could measure up to his music and all the memories I had tied up in it. So, when we saw him standing around at SXSW (Austin's springtime indie rock fest), Pete literally had to push me to talk to him about the cookbook. Turns out, Eric has worked in restaurants all his life. He loves to cook, and he mentioned this seared tuna dish, which, by the way, is ridiculously easy to make and very impressive. When he e-mailed me the recipe, it came with a note that said, "Thanks for allowing me to be a part of your project . . . it's a real honor." The pleasure is all mine.

INGREDIENTS:

1 cup uncooked white rice

1 red bell pepper

olive oil

2 big handfuls of fresh spinach leaves that
  have been washed carefully

1 garlic clove, minced

1 tablespoon white wine vinegar

$1/4$ cup unsweetened coconut milk

2–3 tablespoons sugar

2–3 tablespoons wasabi powder

6- to 8-ounce cut of sashimi-grade tuna

shredded coconut and/or parsley (for
  garnish)

DIRECTIONS:

1. Make white rice according to the directions on the package . . . Set aside . . .

2. Roast the red pepper. (To do this, remove the burner on a gas stove and hold the pep-per with tongs over the open flame until its skin blackens—and open your windows to let out the fumes. If you don't have a gas stove, fire up your broiler, cut the pepper in half, and place it skin-side up on a cookie sheet under the broiler. Once the skin is black, let it cool.) Set aside . . .

3. Add a tablespoon or two of olive oil to a pan, and sauté spinach with a little fresh minced garlic and some white wine vinegar . . .

4. Towel-dry cooked spinach (so that when you add it to the rice, the moisture in the cooked spinach doesn't make the rice sticky) . . . set aside to let the spinach dry fur-ther . . .

5. Cut up the roasted red pepper into bite-sized pieces and add to rice . . .

6. Add spinach to the rice and fluff the rice, mixing the red pepper, rice, and spinach into an attractive pilaf . . . set aside . . . on a low burner if you'd like to keep it warm . . . keep an eye on it so it doesn't overcook or scorch . . .

7. Pour about $1/4$ cup of coconut milk into a sauté pan . . .

8. Add equal parts sugar and wasabi powder (around two or three tablespoons each . . . whatever your taste) to the coconut milk as you gradually increase heat to allow the sugar and wasabi to melt into the coconut milk . . . be careful not to scorch . . . set aside . . . over low heat to keep warm . . . careful not to let the sauce break up . . . not too much heat . . .

9. Over high heat . . . in a cast-iron skillet . . . with a touch of olive oil if you like . . . pan-sear the tuna . . . rare . . . or to your liking . . .

10. Put the rice pilaf onto a plate . . . put the tuna on top of the rice . . . and ladle some of the wasabi-coconut sauce over the tuna . . . shredded coconut makes a nice garnish on this one . . . as does parsley.

Serves 2.

from Eirik Glambek Boe

WOLF FISH *À L'ITALIA*

Kings of Convenience write pretty, lilting melodies that even your mother would love—they sound a bit like Simon & Garfunkel, only stripped down, quieter, and Norwegian. Their fish of choice, though, is an incredibly hideous and menacing undersea creature, which can be found off Norway's northern shores. Wolf fish have sharp, snaggly teeth and jaws powerful enough to bite through mussel shells, or fishermen's fingers, as the case may be, and full-grown wolf fish weigh in at a beastly forty-five pounds. Scary as they may sound, they're very popular in Scandinavian kitchens for their firm meat, which is perfect for stir-fries. But unless you have a Viking friend who can spear a wolf fish for you, your best bet is to substitute catfish fillet into this elegant minimalist dish.

HERE'S WHAT I HAD FOR DINNER TONIGHT (IT'S TRUE) . . .

INGREDIENTS:

10-ounce wolf fish (or catfish) fillet, cubed

salt

4–5 tablespoons tasty olive oil

5 tomatoes, chopped

2 garlic cloves, 1 chopped and one
    squeezed through a garlic press

2 big handfuls of fresh spinach leaves

$1/2$ pound of whole wheat spaghetti (or
    pasta of choice)

red wine (for drinking)

DIRECTIONS:

1. cut 10-ounce fish fillet in cubes, add a pinch of salt.
2. put 2 tablespoons of the oil in the frying pan and place it over high heat.
3. briefly fry the cubes at max temperature on both sides.
4. add 5 chopped tomatoes and the chopped garlic cloves.
5. turn down the temperature to low.

6. add more salt.

7. stir when you feel like it—don't let the fish stick to the pan.

meanwhile in another frying pan . . .

8. add a tablespoon or two of olive oil, and the squeezed garlic clove.

9. fry plenty of fresh spinach leaves at medium temperature. (I think this is a vietnamese dish called "morning glory," but it goes well with italian food).

10. boil some interesting pasta, like for example whole wheat spaghetti. follow the instructions on the box.

11. add more of the tasty olive oil.

12. serve with red wine.

Serves 2.

from Ben Sterling

TROPICAL FISH TACOS

As you may remember from your middle-school math class, a Mobius band is a surface with only one edge and only one side that can be made by cutting a strip of paper, twisting it one hundred eighty degrees, and then taping it into a loop. The band called Mobius Band is even more fun than a craft break in the middle of your first algebra course—they're a trio who moved to Brooklyn from the tiny town of Shutesbury, Massachusetts, and they play catchy pop with understated electronic undertones. In this recipe, vocalist Ben Sterling brightens his fish tacos with honey and pineapple. I like to pile on some hot sauce to balance the natural sweetness.

> "on tour, the most interesting we get is the peanut butter sandwich. occasionally, this also features jelly, though that implies the kind of refrigeration that an econoline cannot afford. but when i get home sometimes it's time to actually fend for myself. few ingredients and minimal clean-up is a chief concern."
>
> —BEN STERLING

INGREDIENTS:

a few limes

honey

some white fish (flounder, tilapia, anything)

scallions

red pepper

pineapple

lettuce

corn tortillas

DIRECTIONS:

1. squeeze a few limes and pour some honey into something you can mix them around in with a spoon. the honey will not want to mate with the lime at first. but it will.

2. coat the fish with honey-lime sauce. let it sit while you prepare the vegetables and pineapple.

3. cut up scallions, red pepper, and pineapple. saute together with a little honey until the scallions and pepper are as soft as you wish.

4. broil the fish. probably not for that long. 5 minutes-ish.

5. cut up some lettuce into strips.

6. assemble it all in your favorite corn tortilla. you can grill the tortillas for a minute if you so desire, i usually do.

One pound of fish serves 3–4.

from Patrick himself

SWANKY MAC AND CHEESE

Singer-songwriter Patrick Phelan crafts dreamy, lingering music, studies human rights, and has spent time in Italy to focus on his cooking, as he has been a chef for more than eleven years. This decadent dish is something you should save for a special occasion because (a) you're going to have to drop a lot of cash to make it happen, (b) you're going to need to kill a pair of lobsters in the process, and (c) it'll make your special day that much more special. This is a challenging recipe, but if you follow the directions carefully, you'll end up with a dish that's as fancy as it is comforting—and big enough to feed a crowd. If you're cooking for two, just make half—you'll still savor the leftovers for lunch the next day.

"This recipe comes courtesy of the great influences of David Shannon, one of my many teachers over the years."

—PATRICK PHELAN

INGREDIENTS:

1 bunch asparagus

2 pounds medium shell pasta

olive oil

two 1 1/2–2 pound lobsters

1/2 cup each of celery, onions, and
　　carrots

2 cups fontina cheese

1 cup Gruyère cheese

1 1/2 cups white wine

1 bay leaf

1 1/2 quarts heavy cream

salt and pepper

white truffle oil

3–4 slices of white truffle (optional)

1. In a large pot of well-salted boiling water, blanch asparagus. (That is, dump the aspara-gus into boiling water for just a minute, and then take them out with some tongs and put them in a colander. Run cold water over them so they stop cooking.) Use the same water to cook your pasta, according to package directions. Toss a little olive oil into the cooked pasta so it does not stick together and set aside.

2. In a large pot of boiling water, cook lobsters for approximately 6–8 minutes. When shells are bright red, remove from water, and place in ice water or run under cold water to stop the lobster from cooking any further. Remove claws, shoulder, and tail meat, and set aside.

3. Dice celery, onions, and carrots, grate fontina and Gruyère cheeses, and set aside.

SAUCE:

1. In a large pot, sauté diced veggies in olive oil.

2. When veggies become translucent pour in white wine and add your bay leaf. Let the wine reduce by half and then add the heavy cream. Let the cream come just to a simmer and reduce to medium heat.

3. After this reduces for approximately 20 minutes, add both cheeses (reserve a little for later). Make sure to stir frequently. You want the sauce just hot enough to melt the cheese, but if it gets any hotter, you'll run the risk of the cream and oils separating.

4. Once the cheese is incorporated, season with salt and pepper to your liking. Go easy on the salt, though—it does not take much to release the flavor of this cheese sauce. You can use white or black pepper, whichever you prefer.

5. After seasoning, strain the cheese sauce through a medium-to-small mesh sieve or colander.

TO THE BOWL:

1. In a large sauté or baking pan over medium heat, add your cheese sauce and lobster. Once heated add your pasta and the little bit of cheeses you reserved. You should get a nice mac and cheese consistency. You can always add more cheese.

2. The final step is to add sliced asparagus just before plating. This will ensure that they remain nice and green.

3. Once the mac and cheese is in the bowl, here's your final touch, and the most important! Drizzle a modest amount of truffle oil over the entire dish. If you do have access to white truffles, 3–4 slices on top is divine. Enjoy.

Serves 8–10.

from RJ Krohn

FISH TACOS WITH AVOCADOS

When RJD2 isn't going solo, he's the hip-hop producer in Soul Position, a joint-project with emcee and fellow Columbus, Ohio, resident, Blueprint. His music echoes the sophistication of DJ Shadow's sound-scapes, but he peppers them with elements that are purely his own—like classic soul samples and sci-fi sound effects. Here, he presents an original mash-up for your kitchen. Pulverizing a beautiful tilapia fillet with a packet of taco seasoning may seem like a bad idea, but trust RJ on this one. The seasoning overrides the tilapia's mellow flavor, and the tacos taste like they're filled with magically light and grease-free ground beef. For his next trick, RJ melts the cheese in the taco shells. Brilliant.

"Me and my better half have a go-to meal when you need a taco, but don't want the beef. Come to think of it, I'm Mr. Mom at home, so this is really my baby. Anyway, fish tacos as follows . . ."   —RJD2

INGREDIENTS:

2 tablespoons olive oil

2 fillets of white fish, such as tilapia
    (about 1 pound total)

salt and pepper

6 taco shells

1 avocado

1 teaspoon fresh lemon juice

packet of taco seasoning

grated taco cheese

lettuce

salsa

tortilla chips

DIRECTIONS:

1. olive oil in a skillet. when hot, throw two fillets of white fish, tilapia preferably, in the pan. salt and pepper 'em. after about two or three minutes, flip the fillets and cook the other side for another two minutes and take off the heat.

2. put taco shells on a cookie sheet and into an oven set to 250°F or so, and keep checking on them to avoid burnt shells.

3. take one avocado—cut in half, peel/de-seed, and scoop innards into a small bowl. listen, cuz you gotta get this right. a good dash of salt, a good dash of pepper, but a TINY amount of lemon juice. a teaspoon. easy to fuck up with too much lemon juice. mash together, perfect guacamole.

4. when fish is done, add taco seasoning from packet. chop it all up so it looks like puke.

5. heat shells in oven 5 min, take out, put cheese in, heat again for 3 min.

6. chop up some lettuce real fine and put some salsa in a bowl.

7. shovel the fish into the shells, top with lettuce, and serve with guacamole and chips. voilà!

Serves 2.

from Camu Tao

ROOFTOP PARTY SALMON

S.A. Smash is a hip-hop duo with a DIY sound on the indie hip-hop label Definitive Jux. (You may also know it as "Def Jux," but they changed their name after they achieved multi-platinum success and the folks at Def Jam ordered a cease and desist.) Producer and solo artist El-P runs the label and throws regular parties for the Definitive Jux family on his Brooklyn rooftop, which led to the genesis of this recipe. According to S.A. Smash's publicist, Kathryn Frazier, "Camu Tao of the group is sort of famous in indie hip-hop for his cooking and makes this weekly at El-P's house!"

INGREDIENTS:

6-ounce salmon fillet (about an inch thick)
Salt & pepper, to taste
Oregano
Organic garlic & herb marination
     (marinade)

Butter
Chili Sauce (God Sauce)/believe it's
     Vietnamese . . .

DIRECTIONS:

1. Chop the salmon into thick sticks with the grain, pat the salt, pepper, & oregano onto the top part of the meat, and marinate in the garlic & herb sauce overnight.
2. Morning. You wake up and say this is going to be cracking, you put 2 tablespoons of butter under fish in an aluminum foil wrap and spread God Sauce on top and let it bake in the oven at 400°F, or on the grill over medium heat, for 15 minutes, flipping the fillets halfway through. Make sure not to burn it.

Serves 1—multiply for a crowd.

from Judah Nagler

SPAGHETTI WITH CLAM CHOWDER SAUCE

The parking lot of a pub at lunchtime is always an odd setting for a show, but it was an especially strange place to hear Santa Rosa, California's the Velvet Teen unveil their experimental post-*Elysium* sound. Laptop-generated noise replaced vocalist Judah Nagler's keyboards and guitar, while drummer Casey Deitz and bassist Josh Staples worked a mystifying off-time groove. Despite the widened eyes of everyone in the parking lot, Judah still looked sleepy after the performance. He grinned shyly when I mentioned his two-ingredient pasta, and Ezra Caraeff, who runs their label, Slowdance, seemed appalled by the recipe. "No, it's really good," Judah said, defensively. "It's my cheap *Alfredo*!" It's actually more like clam sauce, especially if you season it with basil, oregano, garlic power, and a few shakes of red pepper flakes, but Judah is content to eat it plain.

INGREDIENTS:

One pound of pasta

One big can of clam chowder (red or white is fine)

DIRECTIONS:

1. Boil the pasta.
2. Drain it.
3. Put it in a bowl and pour the soup on it.
4. Eat.

Serves 4.

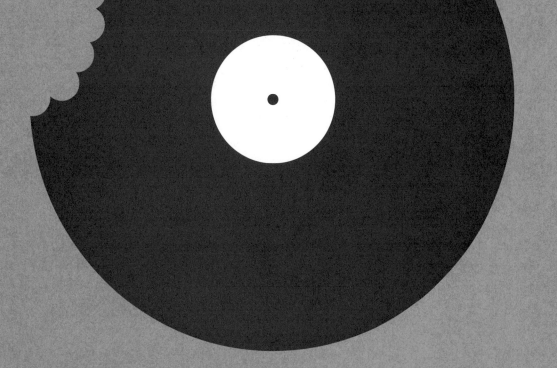

MAIN COURSES FOR VEGETARIANS | FIVE

EATING ON THE road can be a bummer for anybody, but the endless string of fast-food joints along America's highways looks a lot more dismal if you don't eat meat. Even if you're a Taco Bell fan, it's hard to imagine a crueler culinary fate than a month of bean burritos. A few of the recipes in this chapter were developed specifically for on-the-road consumption, in hopes of easing the bean-eater's pain. Kudzu Wish's ingenious Curry Variations uses one basic curry sauce, but varies the other ingredients to keep things interesting, meal after meal. The Quick Chickpeas from Now It's Overhead are spiked with nutritional yeast and liquid amino acids to replenish the nutrients missing from a limited vegetarian diet, and they can be spread on toast or stuffed into bell peppers for a little change of pace. Elizabeth Elmore from the Reputation travels with a mini-kitchen and turns veggie burgers, brown rice, and egg substitute into a stir-fry for that rare creature—the vegetarian who hates vegetables.

Other recipes in this chapter were engineered as post-tour food. Dave Lerner, bassist for Ted Leo and the Pharmacists shares the semi-raw pasta he created as part of a detox diet. Gavin Dunbar from Camera Obscura, after traveling through Spain and watching others happily consume heaping plates of meaty paella, was inspired to cook up a vegetarian-friendly version to enjoy when he got back home. Voxtrot's Peanutty Black-Bean Tofu was created out of desperation for a home-cooked meal with the scant ingredients leftover in drummer Matt Simon's hometown kitchen—and has since become a favorite supper at his house.

A few recipes in this chapter (and sprinkled throughout the book) are as much about sustenance as they are about dining companionship. They include the black bean nachos that Thor Harris from Shearwater makes at band practice, the vegetable enchiladas Matt Pond shares with his roommate (when she isn't giving him the silent treatment for messing up her shopping order), the mac and cheese that Mark Rozzo of Maplewood whips up for his wife the night before he leaves for tour, and the spinach lasagna that Brian Venable from Lucero carefully layers for his girlfriend and her kids. Even John Darnielle of the Mountain Goats, who built a career on songs about troubled love affairs, shows his romantic side with a heart-warming budget dinner recipe, devised for his wife.

from Reid Anderson

ORECCHIETTE WITH BROCCOLI RABE

The Bad Plus is neither an indie band nor a rock band, but they're definitely the most indie-rock jazz trio you'll ever encounter. With their experimental-yet-infectious sound, they're sort of the Sonic Youth of the jazz world. Their originals are like music from the future—grand, audacious, and a few steps ahead of everyone else. Their catalogue of covers includes songs from Nirvana, Blondie, Aphex Twin, Björk, and even the theme from *Chariots of Fire*, and they blow each one up into a larger-than-life, blissed-out riot. I'd say that they rock really hard for a jazz band, but the truth is, they rock really hard—period.

Here, stand-up bass player Reid Anderson shares a rustic Southern Italian pasta dish. "*Orecchiette*" is the Italian word for "little ears" and also for this ear-shaped pasta. Broccoli rabe, or *rapini*, is a slightly bitter leafy green that's most widely available in springtime. (I think it's pretty delicious, but my father, who isn't a big fan of green vegetables anyway, really hates it. He shudders when he recalls how his Sicilian-born grandfather used to grow the stuff in their backyard.) If you like, you can balance the bitterness of the broccoli rabe by tossing in a handful of whole grape tomatoes when you add the garlic. Vegetarians can skip the anchovies, but don't skimp on the freshly grated Parmesan cheese.

> "This is a staple of mine whenever I have access to broccoli rabe." —REID ANDERSON

INGREDIENTS:

1 lb. *orecchiette* pasta (penne works well also)

1 bunch broccoli rabe

Extra-virgin olive oil

2–3 cloves garlic, chopped fine

2–3 anchovy fillets (optional)

Salt and fresh ground pepper

Crushed red pepper

Grated Parmigiano-Reggiano cheese

1. Cook pasta.

2. Blanch broccoli rabe in salted water for about 15 seconds, remove, and drain.

3. Heat olive oil in a pan over medium-low heat and add the garlic.

4. When garlic starts to brown, add the anchovy fillets (if using) and break them apart in the pan for a minute or two.

5. Add the drained broccoli rabe and sauté for a couple minutes.

6. Add salt to taste.

7. Add crushed red pepper to taste.

8. Add sautéed broccoli rabe to the pasta and mix to distribute evenly.

9. Serve with fresh ground pepper and grated Parmigiano-Reggiano cheese.

Serves 4.

from Gavin Dunbar

VEGETARIAN PAELLA

A traditionally meaty Spanish dish turned vegetarian by a bass player in a Scottish indie pop band may not sound all that promising, but Camera Obscura's Gavin Dunbar is going to surprise you. I tested this recipe on a day when I was planning on eating alone— I didn't anticipate a crowd-pleaser—but just as the aromas of garlic and saffron began to fill my kitchen, my boyfriend stopped by. He tasted some rice right from the pan and asked, "Why did you make this without calling me first?" Oops. Next time, I'll make enough Vegetarian Paella to share, and I'll pair it with some Spanish wine, olives, and the Scoville Tortilla Espanola for a meatless Spanish feast. If you're using sausage instead of tofu and want to keep this vegan, be sure to use a brand like Tofurky that says "certified-vegan" on the label.

"We've been playing in Spain a fair bit in the last few years. Our label is based in Madrid, and it's been really nice going over and getting to try out different foods. Spanish cooking is big on rice, and their tortillas certainly beat Scottish omelets any day. The only drawback is that there isn't a great deal of choice if you are vegetarian because the culture is very big on meat. So, on returning to Glasgow armed with cheap Spanish saffron, I thought it might be nice to try and make paella using a veggie option rather than just making it with rice and vegetables. Tofu works really well, especially if you get marinated tofu—you can use any meat-free substitute, though, Quorn or whatever. My personal favourite is using Linda McCartney veggie sausages, 'cause they taste great and have a really good texture."

—GAVIN DUNBAR

INGREDIENTS:

2 tablespoons olive oil

1 large onion (chopped)

1 clove of garlic (minced)

1 red pepper

1 green pepper

1 pack of tofu (or veggie sausage, cut into bite-size pieces)

1 cup of paella rice (short grain)

pinch of saffron

1 teaspoon of turmeric

10-ounce package of frozen peas

2 cups of vegetable stock

DIRECTIONS:

1. Heat the olive oil in a pan, then sauté the onion with the garlic.

2. Add in chopped peppers and chopped up tofu (you can also use chopped up veggie sausages).

3. Add in the rice, a pinch of saffron, and a teaspoon of turmeric and continue to heat for five minutes.

4. Add the vegetable stock and the peas and stir frequently as you cook slowly on a low heat for half an hour, or until the stock has reduced away.

Serves 2.

from Victoria Bergsman

TOMATO SAUCE FOR PASTA

English is not the first language of the Concretes, an adorable pop octet from Stockholm, Sweden, who are named for their love of urban architecture. Thus, this simple yet satisfying recipe came with a disclaimer from the band that read: "Here comes a recipe from the Concretes own cook, Victoria! There might be many wrong spellings and strange words. Get back to us if you do not understand it." I only found two strange words here, but I left them in so that you can add them to your culinary vocabulary: "garnation," the act of decorating a finished dish; and "chilipepperfruits," a far cuter term for "hot peppers."

INGREDIENTS:

4–6 tomatoes or a can of whole tomatoes (if you find some nice italian canned tomatoes)

2–3 garlic cloves

2–3 small dried chilipepperfruits (also known as *piri-piri*)

2 tablespoonfuls of nice olive oil

1–2 tablespoonfuls of butter

1 pound of pasta (plain is fine, but fresh ravioli is better)

$1/2$ teaspoonful of salt (you can add more, to taste, but remember that parmesan is quite salty, which you add in the end . . .)

1 tablespoonful of sugar

2 handfuls of fresh basil, minced (save some for garnation)

2 cupfuls parmesan cheese (save $1/3$ cup for serving)

DIRECTIONS:

1. wash the tomatoes and boil them (if you choose fresh tomatoes) in water, so they are covered. let them boil for a minute (to make the skin come off easier). throw them over into a colander and leave them under cold running water for a minute so you don't burn your fingers. then peel the skin off.

2. mince the garlic cloves & chilifruits.

3. heat a frying pan or a saucepan and pour in the oil and the butter. wait till the butter has melted then fry the garlic and chili while stirring it all the time on full heat for a few minutes.

4. then remove it from the heat while chopping the tomatoes (into small squares), and then put them into the pan. let it cook gently for 5–10 minutes (lower the heat a little) or so until everything is mushed together.

5. now is a good time to put on water for the pasta to boil. use a big pan 'cause pasta demands a lot of water and salt the water generously. preferably use fresh pasta, maybe spinach and ricotta ravioli . . . or just plain pasta, choose your favourite.

6. back to the sauce . . . now add the salt and sugar, stir. add the minced basil and stir. finally add the grated parmesan cheese and stir.

7. make sure to take the pasta off almost too early rather than too late 'cause it will stay kind of warm being mixed with the warm tomato sauce, and you don't want the pasta to get too spongy.

8. place the pasta into some big glass bowl or whatever and then pour over the sauce and mix it together. carefully sprinkle over the rest of the cheese and put some basil leaves on top and serve immediately!

WE DO HOPE YOU ENJOY IT.

LOVE /The Concretes

Serves 4.

from Victoria "Rifle" Pilato

BAKED BARBECUE TOFU

Vicki Pilato may seem shy and timid at Heston Rifle shows as she cowers in the corner of the stage, but she's actually just trying to avoid getting whacked by one of her fellow band members' thrashing guitars. The boys play like thunder, and the enchanting sound of her violin is like an eerie calm in the storm. There's also some magic in her cooking methods—I don't know what kind of chemical reaction happens to frozen and defrosted tofu, but somehow, it helps Vicki cook up substantial, un-mushy tofu without the use of a frying pan. This is super with barbecue sauce, but if you can take the heat, it's also worth trying with the hot sauce from Windsor for the Derby's Spicy Wings à la Chickie.

"I try to bring lunch to work but I get bored really fast with whatever I come up with. I tried those veggie deli slices and baked flavored tofu from the market (I'm a veggie-tarian person if you haven't guessed) to make sandwiches, but they taste bad and the tofu is really messy and only flavorful on the outside with mushy tofu on the inside. Yuck! I decided to make my own baked tofu recipe the way I thought it should be. This not only works great in sandwiches but also cut up in a salad.

"This recipe calls for tofu that was frozen and then fully defrosted. You can freeze and defrost the tofu in its package. It might take more than a day to fully defrost. This process leaves the tofu with a spongier texture, which leads to more flavor absorption." —VICTORIA "RIFLE" PILATO

INGREDIENTS:

1 tablespoon vegetable oil

1-pound package of firm or extra-firm organic tofu in water (frozen and thawed)

1 bottle of your favorite barbecue sauce (mine is Consorzio Organic BBQ Sauce Original)

EQUIPMENT:

cookie sheet

1. Preheat oven to 350°F.
2. Grease the cookie sheet with the oil. Use a paper towel to spread oil around the pan making sure it is completely covered. Only a light covering is needed to prevent tofu from sticking (no oily puddles).
3. Take the defrosted tofu out of the package and discard the water.
4. Press the tofu block a bunch of times to get the excess water out.
5. Cut ¼-inch slices from the short side of the tofu block
6. Dip each slice in the barbecue sauce, covering it completely. Don't be stingy! (I use almost half the bottle.)
7. Place slices on greased cookie sheet.
8. Bake for 10 minutes.* Take pan out to flip each slice over (I use a fork). Then bake for an additional 10 minutes.

   Store uneaten baked tofu slices in the refrigerator for up to week.

VARIATIONS:

Use any marinade and experiment. It's so easy!

Makes about 4 sandwiches or salads,
depending on how much tofu you use.

---

*This timing is for drier, more manageable tofu you can eat with your hands if you'd like. It's great for sandwiches. If saucier and softer is more to your liking, take a few minutes off the baking time for each side.

from Pete D'Angelo

EGGPLANT PARMESAN

A couple of years ago, instrumental rock quartet Houston McCoy played a show in a very small room in the basement of New York's Knitting Factory. Afterward, my boyfriend, Pete, who plays guitar in the band, said that their other guitarist, Clark, caught me handing out earplugs before their set, and was very hurt. Truth be told, I always hand out earplugs before their shows because they are so awesomely loud that even the thickest, ugliest, hot orange earplugs cannot begin to cancel out their sound. Plus, Pete stands right next to the speakers and refuses to wear earplugs, so I'll need to hear for both of us when he inevitably goes deaf. I share earplugs with my friends so that they will still be able to chat with me when we are old and feeble and my beloved Pete is watching closed-caption TV. Anyway, I'm a bit biased, but I think Houston McCoy is one of the most inspiring, uplifting, and triumphant bands around. They have the coolest makeshift light show and a portable smoke machine, too. And while I'm raving, I'll say that this is the best eggplant parm I've ever tasted. Believe the hype.

"Our drummer, Neil, feels that this dish does not fully represent him as he's averse to eggplant in all forms. Fact is, this is not your usual eggplant dish, and the whole point is to circumvent the creepy mouth-feel you get from undercooked, squishy eggplant. Many a doubtful diner has been forced into trying this meal, but even if they don't like eggplant, they ask for seconds when they eat this. The first time I tried to make this, I had to call my Grandma and Aunt Rae to get some tips—trust me, the Egg Beaters and the brand-name bread crumbs DO drastically improve the flavor." —PETE D'ANGELO

2 medium-sized eggplants

One 3-pack of little (12-ounce) cartons of
Egg Beaters (or 3–4 eggs, if Egg
Beaters are not available)

milk

1 container of Progresso ITALIAN Style
Bread Crumbs

olive oil

Two 26-ounce jars of sauce (You can
usually get some sort of deal from a
brand like Classico, which has all sorts
of awesome flavors. I like to get two
different ones, including one of the
spicier varieties, though if you want a
more puritan delight I'm sure you can
just double up the red sauce.)

One 16-ounce package of whole milk
mozzarella (store brand is fine)

1 bunch of fresh basil

oregano

salt

pepper

1 small fresh smoked mozzarella

TOOLS:

1 large skillet

1 rectangular baking dish

1 apron! (you're gonna be frying here and I
would hate you to ruin that nice shirt)

1 spatula

1 awesome knife

OK, HERE'S HOW THIS GOES . . .

DIRECTIONS:

1. I don't peel the eggplant. Some folks find the skin unnecessary, but in this context, it's not really a problem. Get your awesomely sharp knife (but be careful) and start slicing the eggplant into round slices about $1/2$ to $1/4$ of an inch thick. If you make them too big they're gonna be harder to cook through, so err on the side of thinness.

2. Set up a little station for yourself by the stove top. In one bowl, put your first container of Egg Beaters. I don't really get why they taste different, but Grandma swears by them, so we're just gonna take her word. Throw a little splash of milk in there if you've got some to spare, you'll get a little more mileage out of the mixture that way. Get a large plate next to the bowl and give it a liberal covering with the bread crumbs. Both the eggs and the bread crumbs will likely need to be replenished as this process goes on—just fill 'em back up when resources are low.

3. Get some oil sizzling in the frying pan—$^1/_2$ an inch or so, at most. Keep the heat strong till it pops when you flick some water on it, and you are ready to fry. Everything tastes better fried, but frying everything will kill you. That said, it's a tasty way to go.

4. Take a slice of eggplant, fully submerge in the Egg Beaters, let the excess drain off, and then drop it in the bread crumbs, flipping around until it's fully coated. Then drop it carefully into the oil and repeat with the next slice. You can usually get a handful of pieces in there at a time, but this does take a little while. Leave the eggplant in the pan until it is fried golden brown and decently crisp. If you don't fry it long enough, this meal is going to be mush, and you have a lot of eggplant, so if you overcook a few it's no big deal. Drain the fried pieces on a plate with a paper towel, and repeat ad infinitum, making more layers with more paper towels; this will keep the earlier batches warm.

5. Get out your baking tray and line the bottom with a single layer of eggplant slices. On top of each slice, spoon a big glob of sauce. Top the sauce with a thin slice of the store-brand mozzarella, and top that with a fresh basil leaf. Repeat for all the pieces on that layer. Then sprinkle the whole layer with oregano and some salt and pepper. Cover this all with another layer of eggplant and do it over and over again until you are out of egg-plant and have reached the top of the tray. For this final layer, things are a bit different.

6. For the top layer, you can finish off whatever sauce you have left. Go ahead and dump it on there. Now, instead of the store cheese, open up the fresh smoked mozzarella and slice that thin. Cover up the top of the tray and try to arrange the pieces over the circles of eggplant—it'll make cutting it easier. This cheese melts a little better so it's a nice way to finish things off. Give it another dash of salt and pepper, and you're almost done.

7. Throw the whole tray in the oven at 350°F for about 20 minutes. You want the cheese to get melted, but everything is already cooked so you're pretty safe. I usually stick my finger in the middle of it to see if it's hot all the way through, but that's disgusting and if anyone is looking at you, it may jeopardize their chances of enjoying this meal.

8. Serve with a bottle of red wine and a big loaf of crusty Italian bread. (If you have the choice between seeded and unseeded bread, always get the seeded!) If you don't like this, you are never going to like eggplant.

Serves 4–6.

from Jone Stebbins

EDDIE VEDDER STEW

"This is one of my favorite recipes to whip up for a crowd," says bassist Jone Stebbins, of this vegan dish with a cannibalistic title. Although Imperial Teen's signature brand of sassy and trashy boy-girl pop opposed the grunge movement of the late '90's, the Californian quartet attests that they never attempted to eat a flannel-clad lead singer for dinner. Jone explains, "It's nicknamed Eddie Vedder Stew because he was at a party once at my house and ate several bowlfuls."

INGREDIENTS:

2 tablespoons olive oil

1 cup chopped onion

2 tablespoons garlic, minced

1 1/2 tablespoons curry power

6 carrots, halved and cut into 1-inch
     chunks

3 russet potatoes, cut into 1/2-inch dice

1 medium cauliflower, chopped

4 cups vegetable broth

2 tablespoons honey

1 cinnamon stick

One 15-ounce can of chickpeas (gar-
     banzo beans), drained

2 cups plum tomatoes, chopped, or a
     14.5-ounce can of crushed tomatoes

Cilantro leaves (for garnish)

DIRECTIONS:

Heat oil in large heavy pot. Add onion and sauté for 10 minutes. Stir in garlic and cook 2–3 minutes more. Sprinkle with curry powder and cook for one more minute, stirring to mellow flavors. Add carrots, potatoes, cauliflower, broth, honey, and cinnamon stick, and bring to a boil. Then reduce heat and simmer for 20 minutes. Add chickpeas and tomatoes, and simmer 15 minutes more. Garnish with cilantro.

Serves 4.

from Timothy LaFollette

CURRY VARIATIONS

Greensboro, North Carolina's notorious punk rock five-piece, Kudzu Wish, disbanded when their drummer joined the Peace Corps, but they will retain their place in indie-rock history as some of the most efficient tour chefs who've ever roamed the open road. They always managed to eat healthily on just a couple of dollars a day by packing their van with a fifteen-pound bag of basmati rice and a stockpile of canned beans. The rice cooker that was meant to plug into their cigarette lighter didn't end up working properly, so they'd take over kitchens across the country—feeding themselves and their hosts with bean burritos on rushed days and one of these curries when there was enough time to let it simmer. The great thing about curry is, once you have the sauce, you can add almost anything you (or the people you're crashing with) have on hand. You can go vegan or meaty (if you're not adverse to meat products), hot or not. Here, executive chef and bassist Tim LaFollette offers one basic curry sauce and three sample recipes to use it in. Serve them all over rice, prepared according to package directions.

BASIC CURRY SAUCE

INGREDIENTS:

2 tablespoons of olive oil

1 really big friggin' Vidalia or yellow onion, chopped

1 can of tomato paste

2–4 heaping tablespoons of store-bought curry paste, like Patak's

DIRECTIONS:

1. Warm oil in a large, heavy skillet over medium-high heat.
2. Sauté onion in olive oil until onion is soft, approximately 6 minutes.
3. Stir in tomato paste.
4. Add curry paste, to taste.

Makes approximately 1 cup.

INGREDIENTS:

Basic Curry Sauce

Any vegetables and protein that you have
    on hand, like chickpeas, eggplant,
    peppers, broccoli, cauliflower, zucchini,
    carrots, tempeh, tofu, or chicken strips,
    if you're into meat (To serve 6,
    use 1 1/2 pounds of protein and 4 to 6
    cups of chopped vegetables.)

Peanut butter

Water

2 cups (or 14 ounces) of Basmati rice,
    prepared according to package directions

DIRECTIONS:

1. Add chopped vegetables and protein to heated Basic Curry Sauce.
2. Add peanut butter for a nutty flavor and extra protein.
3. Simmer for at least 30 minutes, stirring occasionally.
4. Add water in small increments if the sauce gets too thick. Serve over rice.

Serves 6.

TIM CURRY

INGREDIENTS:

3 large sweet potatoes, cleaned and cubed

2 pounds of firm tofu

2 tablespoons of olive oil

1 batch of Basic Curry Sauce

1 can of coconut milk

2 cups (or 14 ounces) of Basmati rice,
    prepared according to package
    directions

DIRECTIONS:

1. Cook sweet potatoes in medium-sized pot of boiling water until tender, about 15 minutes.
2. Meanwhile, rinse and drain the tofu, and cut into bite-sized pieces. Heat the olive oil in a large *nonstick* skillet and add the tofu. (Tofu is a bastard when it comes to sticking.) Sauté for about 5 minutes, or until the tofu is golden brown, and then put aside.

3. Try to find a really big pot—this recipe generally fills a wok pan to capacity, so a cauldron-sized pot is probably necessary. This is meant to serve many. Add the Basic Curry Sauce, coconut milk, potatoes, and tofu to the pot and simmer for at least half an hour, or longer if possible. The more time you've got, the better the flavor will be.

4. If the sauce becomes too thick, thin it out with water. Serve over rice.

Serves 6.

BOMBAY TIM'S HOT-ASS VEGAN CURRY

INGREDIENTS:

1 batch of Basic Curry Sauce

Chili peppers, chopped (make it as hot as you like it)

About 10 ounces of frozen or canned spinach (drain if using canned spinach)

Vegetables and protein of your choice— this is good with red bell peppers, russet potatoes, canned whole tomatoes, peas, and tofu (To serve 6, use 1 1/2 pounds of protein and 4 to 6 cups of chopped vegetables.)

DIRECTIONS:

1. Throw everything in a pot and simmer, adding water if it gets too thick. If you're not cooking for vegans, this is good if you throw in some shrimp a few minutes before you serve it—just give them enough time to cook through, but don't leave them stewing.

Serves 6.

from Kyle Field

UNCLE KYLE'S AVOCADO TACOS

Kyle Field is a daydreamer from Portland, Oregon, with a gently warbling, bird-like voice who has shared the stage with Devendra Banhart as his supporting act, member of his backing band, and as a friend. Listening to his peaceful brand of folk, it seems obvious why the two would get along. Kyle's tunes are so loose, they're almost unhinged, and these avocado tacos of his are as simple as his sound.

> "i promise you, i PROmise you, you can not eat only one of these little angels, for they are as a core sample of the very earth we tread upon. i kid you not, it tastes as if you were eating a slice of garden pie cut straight from the ground."
>
> —KYLE FIELD

INGREDIENTS:

olive oil

4 corn tortillas

1 avocado

1 tablespoon of nutritional yeast

a few splashes of Bragg liquid amino acids

a handful of dandelion greens

a handful of other salads

2 tablespoons of Annie's Goddess Dressing

DIRECTIONS:

1. warm tortillas in a little oil and salt or seasoning if desired.
2. finely dice the avocado so it can be scooped out like giblets into the tortillas, sort of spread it around on each tortilla, then add other ingredients, dividing them evenly among the warmed tortillas.
3. eat an orange after they have digested, after going on a walk. go, glow, grow!

Makes 4 small tacos.

from Brian Venable

SPINACH LASAGNA

In the backyard of a South Austin Mexican restaurant and music venue called Jovita's, Lucero's Ben Nichols and Brian Venable were sipping drinks before a midday show. Ben, looking bleary-eyed from the night before, claimed that he doesn't eat very much, let alone cook, but Brian—who already ate breakfast, read the paper, and went for a run—raised both his heavily tattooed hands and said, "I'm a great cook—just ask my girlfriend and her kids. I cook all the time!" Ben pointed and laughed, "You're gonna be in a cookbook, you nerd." Brian ignored him and whipped out a Palm Pilot to show me a new program he just installed—a drink recipe database. A couple of weeks later, Brian typed me this whole recipe on that little keyboard, proving once again that Lucero is one of the hardest-working bands in the business. Even if you're already a big fan of their rough-and-ready country-punk, one taste of this deceptively meaty vegetarian lasagna—and the idea of Brian carefully putting it together in his Memphis kitchen—is sure to bolster your devotion.

> "You'll need some red sauce for this recipe, but since I haven't learned to make my own very well I cheat and use sauce from a jar. I figure you can use whatever your favorite is . . . I use whichever is on sale."
>
> —BRIAN VENABLE

INGREDIENTS AND UTENSILS:

2 saucepans

10" x 12" Pyrex baking dish

1 large mixing bowl

tin foil

4–6 cups red sauce (two 26-ounce jars)

1 bag fake ground beef

1–2 pinches nutritional yeast

salt

pepper

1 or 2 cloves garlic

1 box lasagna noodles

12 ounces ricotta cheese

2 eggs, slightly beaten	vegetable oil
3/4 cup mozzarella cheese	a bag fresh spinach
3/4 cup Asiago cheese	3/4 cup Parmesan cheese
1/2 teaspoon dried basil	2 tablespoons pine nuts
1/2 teaspoon dried oregano	1 tomato

DIRECTION:

1. Preheat the oven to 350°F. You'll need it later . . .
2. In a saucepan over medium heat, pour in the red sauce, the fake ground beef, and add 1 or 2 pinches of nut(ritional) yeast. I like a lot in mine, but again it depends on your taste. Stir it up and maybe add some salt, pepper, and crunch up one of those garlic cloves and put it in there. Mmmmmmmm!
3. Now while you're heating the red sauce, start some water boiling in the other pot (enough to cover a box of lasagna noodles), maybe a quart or so . . .
4. In the large mixing bowl, add the ricotta cheese, eggs, mozzarella cheese, Asiago cheese, basil, oregano, and the other clove of garlic, crunched up. Stir all that up till it's smooth and set it aside for now.
5. Take that Pyrex dish and smear the bottom and sides with a thin layer of vegetable oil. First, put a layer of red sauce on the bottom. Then add a layer of the ricotta mixture, then a layer of spinach, and finally, cover all that with a layer of noodles. Repeat about three times or until you reach the top of the dish. I usually get about 4 layers if I'm lucky. Save a little red sauce for the top, though . . .
6. Then cover with the Parmesan cheese, and sprinkle the pine nuts over the top. Cover with tin foil and put in the oven. Set the timer for 50 minutes.
7. While you're waiting, go ahead and slice that tomato and have it waiting . . .
8. After the timer goes off, set the oven to broil. Uncover the dish, put the tomato slices on top, and put the whole thing in the broiler till it's brown and crispy on top. Take it out and let it cool and eat it up.

Serves 6–8.

from Mark Rozzo

NIGHT-BEFORE-TOUR MAC AND CHEESE

Maplewood woos fans with breezy three-part harmonies, easygoing acoustic guitars, and sunshiny lyrics about Indian summers and dreamy girls lounging in fields of clover. Think Seals & Crofts meets America at a picnic in a New York City park. After all, though their music sounds like it was composed betwixt doobie hits on the Pacific Coast Highway, these guys aren't a bunch of hippies—singer Mark Rozzo (formerly of Champale) is a dad and magazine editor based in Brooklyn, New York. Like Maplewood's music, his stick-to-your-ribs mac and cheese is super mellow, like a wholesome, grown-up version of your favorite boxed variety. If it's *too* mellow for you, either spice it up with dried basil and oregano, maybe a little garlic powder, and plenty of Frank's hot sauce—or just do yourself a favor and chill out. It's all good, man.

"Here's a recipe for the ultimate night-before-tour comfort food, cribbed (and tweaked the way I like it) from my all-time favorite tour eatery, the wholesome and welcoming Grit in Athens, Georgia, perhaps the world's only vegetarian soul-food restaurant—a place I like to think of as the indie-rock Moosewood. (Although I've heard others call it, appreciatively, the indie-rock Hooters.)

"I like to do this up before heading out on a long trip; the homey ritual of putting it together and sharing it with a loved one or bandmate is the best way to stock up on mellow domestic vibes before you hit the turnpike and spend the coming weeks in a blur of Cracker Barrels and Iron Skillets. It also makes the task of folding and counting T-shirts just a little more manageable. The fun part is carving the bread (please, no multigrain) into suggestive shapes that commemorate the occasion, whether it be your first journey to Tallahassee or Valentine's Day. (You don't need to be a touring band to love Mac and Cheese.)"

—MARK ROZZO

INGREDIENTS:

12 cups water

4 cups (one pound) dried elbow macaroni

6 tablespoons butter, divided

2 large eggs, beaten

4 cups whole milk

1 heaping teaspoon Colman's dry English
    mustard

2 teaspoons salt

pinch of white pepper

pinch of cayenne pepper

1 1/2 tablespoons Tabasco

1 tablespoon Worcestershire sauce

6 cups shredded sharp cheddar

1 small handful grated fresh
    Parmigiano-Reggiano

1 or 2 slices of white sandwich bread OR
    1 1/2 cups unflavored, preferably
    homemade, bread crumbs

DIRECTIONS:

1. Preheat oven to 425°F.

2. Grease a 9" x 13" casserole.

3. Bring water to a boil in a large stockpot and add macaroni. Boil until al dente. Remove and drain in colander.

4. Melt 3 tablespoons butter in pot and add drained macaroni; stir to combine. Meanwhile, whisk together eggs, milk, dry mustard, salt, peppers, Tabasco, and Worcestershire in a bowl.

5. Add mixture to pasta and cheeses and stir constantly over medium-high heat until cheese melts and milk and eggs begin to thicken.

6. Continue cooking, stirring constantly, for 5 minutes or so, or until creamy and thick. Transfer contents of pot to buttered casserole dish.

7. Melt remaining butter in a small saucepan. Trim crust from bread slice(s) and cut into desired shape(s): initial(s) of loved one or band name, numbers of year ("06"), band logo, heart(s), guitars, the shape of Texas, etc.

8. Gently press carved bread slice(s) into top of macaroni mixture and brush with butter. OR Mix melted butter with bread crumbs. Spread crumbs evenly over macaroni mixture. (If using bread slices, a small amount of un-buttered crumbs can be dusted on top of macaroni mixture to absorb moisture and encourage browning.)

9. Optional: Sprinkle grated fresh Parm on top.
10. Bake 10–15 minutes, until golden brown. Use broiler to brown further, if necessary. Pass the sweet tea and Tabasco.

> Note: *This is great the next day, when it congeals into a dense, cheesy gateau.*

Serves 10 to 12.

from Matt Pond himself

VEGETABLE ENCHILADAS WITH HOMEMADE TOMATILLO SALSA

I spent much of the mid-'80s sipping juice boxes in my pink bedroom beneath a canopy of unicorn posters, and spinning singles from the late '60s, such as Bread's "It Don't Matter to Me" and Donovan's "Jennifer Juniper," on a white plastic record player. Now that I'm grown-up and I prefer listening to music in dark clubs and drinking whiskey until the stage lights resemble a hazy rainbow, Matt Pond PA's disarmingly sweet chamber pop fulfills my latent lite-rock cravings, without forcing me to sacrifice my street cred. Matt's music box orchestra plays the prettiest songs, but there's always a sharpness to them, sort of like the passive-aggressive barbs in this otherwise tender and affectionate recipe. It feeds a crowd, but to make it quickly, you'll need a food processor or blender with at least a five-cup capacity to chop the tomatillo salsa. You'll also need two 9" x 13" baking pans to accommodate the 12 enchiladas.

"This recipe almost caused a relationship to end.

"In my apartment, my roommate, Miriam Kienle, is the executive chef and I merely take orders. She's easily achieved this title; her skills have been proven, and I've had the privilege of enjoying tons of incredible meals with incredible wines. Still, there can be something somewhat frustrating about people who seek control, yet lack focus . . . I love you, Miriam.

"Last fall, we decided that we would make a dinner together: vegetarian enchiladas with a tomatillo sauce. I would go fetch the food and cut it into appropriate sizes, and she would cook the food and take credit. There was nothing wrong with this. I hate burning food and having to order Thai . . . but trying to find tomatillos on a Sunday night proved nearly impossible, so get your tomatillos early. (I spent four hours of searching at every grocery store and bodega in northern Brooklyn because Miriam will only have the freshest tomatillo sauce!) So, hours and hours later, we were all eating wearily, hungrily,

ENCHILADAS

INGREDIENTS:

2 red onions

2 green bell peppers

2 red bell peppers

2 small-to-medium zucchini

2 small-to-medium yellow squash

2 tablespoons olive oil

Salt and pepper

16-ounce block (or more) *queso blanco* and/or Jack cheese

12 flour tortillas

TOMATILLO SALSA

INGREDIENTS:

20 fresh tomatillos

1 clove garlic

1 small white onion,

1 fresh jalapeño chili

$1/4$ cup chopped cilantro

1 tablespoon or more lime juice

Salt to taste

DIRECTIONS:

1. Preheat oven to 350°F.
2. Cut onions and bell peppers into $1/4$-inch-thick wedges. Cut zucchini and squash into thin slices. Sauté vegetables in olive oil, sprinkle salt and pepper, and cook until tender. Allow them to cool while you make tomatillo salsa.
3. Husk, wash, and dice tomatillos. Finely chop garlic, onion, jalapeño, and cilantro. Mix tomatillos with everything else and pour in freshly squeezed lime juice. Sprinkle salt to taste. (To save time, use a food processor or blender rather than chopping tomatillos and other items.)

4. Grate or chop the *queso*. Pour a strip of salsa down the middle of a tortilla, cover salsa with cheese, and put veggie mixture on top. Roll up the tortilla and place in a pan or on a cookie sheet that has been rubbed with olive oil. Make each tortilla the same way, and once they are all lined up in the pan, sprinkle cheese and any leftover salsa on top.

5. Bake for 20–30 minutes, or until cheese is browned and bubbly. This dish goes well with beans and rice, and a nice bottle of pinot grigio or cans of Tecate.

Makes 12 enchiladas—enough to feed a small orchestra.

from John Darnielle

TATO MATO

This recipe from John Darnielle of the Mountain Goats, one of the most prolific and talented songwriters of our time, is more than just a recipe. It's a guide to budget cooking, an essay on appreciating life's simple pleasures, and a testimony of his love for his wife—which is even more touching and impressive if you've heard all his songs about embittered relationships. It's also proof that a romantic meal can be prepared for just a couple bucks.

> "When I get home from tour I look forward to cooking for my wife more than almost anything. Sleeping in my own bed, watching television, quiet, peaceful times: these are all good. But fixing dinner for me & my wife is a huge part of my identity, and on tour I feel as though this very important part of me is involuntarily put into hibernation. It takes a day or two to re-acclimate to the kitchen, and then it's time for some Tato Mato."
>
> —JOHN DARNIELLE

INGREDIENTS:

1 cup jasmine or basmati rice

2–3 potatoes

$1/4$-inch of a stick of ghee or butter

1 teaspoon black mustard seeds

1 teaspoon cumin seeds

1–3 tomatoes

10 ounces frozen peas

10 ounces frozen cauliflower

$1/2$ teaspoon oregano

$1/2$ teaspoon basil

pinch of asafoetida

1–2 teaspoons soy sauce or rice vinegar

THE HISTORY OF TATO MATO

When we lived in Colo, Iowa, we were fairly poor. We got by all right because we can be pretty good at pinching pennies when that's what the situation calls for. I knew from previous not-havin'-much-money experience that potatoes are the poor man's best friend.

Lalitree (that's my wife's name, don'tcha know) likes to grow tomatoes, and no matter where you live there's always space for a tomato plant or two. In Iowa the soil's rich and the heat's high in the summer and you get a lot of tomatoes. You see which way this is leading.

TATO MATO: THE FREE JAZZ OF HOME COOKING

1. If you have some potatoes and you have some tomatoes you are better than halfway to a decent dinner. Make some jasmine rice, why don't you? Or basmati if that's your thing. Make about a cup's worth: rinse the rice several times if it's basmati, don't rinse it more than once if it's jasmine, bring to a boil in 2 cups water, reduce heat to very low and cover; when water is absorbed (about 20 minutes), turn off heat and leave to stand for at least 30 minutes. If it stands covered and undisturbed for an hour or so the texture gets very nice. I don't know why.

2. While the rice is standing, cut up some potatoes. I like 'em diced; you may like chip-like slices, or julienne fingers. It's all you, baby! Heat your preferred cooking medium in a frying pan: ghee is the best thing ever, but will make you fat. You should be so blessed as to never have anything worse to worry about than whether you're getting fat, eh? G'head, use the ghee, you'll thank me. Heat about $1/4$ inch of it but don't be a fascist about measurements. Tato Mato is all about the feeling. When it's hot, drop a teaspoon of black mustard seeds and another teaspoon of cumin seeds into it. Stir them, agitate them. Throw in the potatoes, stir to coat, reduce heat to medium low.

3. While the potatoes are cooking, slice you up a nice tomato or 2, or 3, even, depending on a) the size of the tomatoes, b) how much you like that delicious tomato taste, c) whether you actually have three tomatoes on hand. Want other vegetables? Peas are awfully nice. Go ahead and boil some frozen peas in water, and drain them, and set them aside. Cauliflower is a good thing, too, but don't let me pressure you about it. I must say, though, that once the cauliflower hits the ghee, it's good times all around. Once the tomatoes are sliced—I dice them; it's what I recommend—toss them with some oregano and maybe some dried basil. Certainly you'll want to dust them with asafoetida (also known as hing)—go easy on it, it's a strong spice, but don't go so easy

that you can't taste it. Now stir the spice-dusted tomatoes into the cool rice and leave to one side. Add the peas, too, if you used 'em.

4. By now it should be time to flip the potatoes. See how nice and brown they are—how they've gotten a delicious high-fat crust? Oh, wow, this is going to be yummy. If you're using some cauliflower, now's the time to add the florets: You have to watch closely once the cauliflower goes in, 'cause it burns easily, and nobody likes burnt cauliflower. When the cauliflower's done, the potatoes will probably be done, too: So stir in the whole rice/tomato mixture. Add a good teaspoon or two of soy sauce, or maybe some rice vinegar. Don't use both! That'd be too much. Heat to warm, stirring and mixing well.

5. Serve in bowls. Bless the Name. Love the one you're with.

Serves 2.

from Adam Turla

SPICED TOFU STIR-FRY

"Murder by Death" would be the perfect name for a band that follows in the footsteps of metalheads like Slayer, Megadeth, or Cannibal Corpse, but you won't find any growling Cookie Monster vocals here. Lead man Adam Turla sounds a little bit like Nick Cave and a little bit like Johnny Cash, while his band, complete with a cellist, churns out a whiskey-soaked, saloon-style brand of rock 'n' roll. Like Vicki from Heston Rifle, Adam freezes and defrosts his tofu before cooking to improve its texture. This simple stir-fry is great over rice.

"This is a tasty and unique dish that happens to be vegan. The variety of flavors makes for a sweet and spicy stir-fry that also maintains the delicious taste of the golden vegetables. For those unfamiliar with cooking tofu, there are a few guidelines to make it taste its best. First, if you are using it as a meat substitute, always buy extra-firm tofu. Next, if you freeze the tofu and then defrost it in the microwave it will lose a lot of its water and will then brown better, and therefore taste better. After you've prepped it, you can then fry it up."

—ADAM TURLA

INGREDIENTS:

10 ounces tofu

2 teaspoons ground cumin

1 tablespoon paprika

1 teaspoon ground ginger

Cayenne pepper, to taste

1 tablespoon sugar

Salt and pepper, to taste

2/3 cup pine nuts, toasted

4 tablespoons olive oil, separated

2 garlic cloves, crushed

1 bunch scallions

1 red bell pepper, sliced

1 yellow bell pepper, sliced

1 large zucchini, sliced into discs

1 large yellow squash, sliced into discs

1 tablespoon lime juice

1–3 tablespoons maple syrup, depending
   on how sweet you like it

1. Prep tofu as directed above (freeze it and then defrost it in the microwave).
2. Combine cumin, paprika, ginger, cayenne, sugar, salt, and pepper.
3. Cut tofu into cubes and coat in the mixture and save any left.
4. Put half the tofu in a pan, and cook tofu on medium heat until browned. Then, remove the pan from the heat.
5. Toast the pine nuts (in the oven or toaster oven) until browned.
6. Add the remaining oil to the pan and cook garlic and scallions until pale. Then add the remaining vegetables and cook over medium heat until softened and golden. If you have leftover spice mixture, sprinkle it over the vegetables.
7. Return tofu to the pan and add toasted pine nuts, lime juice, and maple syrup. Serve in a bowl.

Serves 4.

from Andy LeMaster

QUICK CHICKPEAS

Onstage, Andy LeMaster of Now It's Overhead sings over slow-burning layers of sound with a big, bold voice that belies his small frame and soft Southern drawl. When I met Andy over a glass of red in a West Village wine bar, I had trouble connecting such a cheerful and chatty person with his intense stage presence. He talked excitedly about touring with Bright Eyes and R.E.M., but explained how tough it is to stay meat- and dairy-free on the road. "Germany is brutal for veganism," he said, "but I'll eat vegetables there, as long as they're not cooked with eyeballs or anything." At home in Athens, Georgia, he uses canned chickpeas and a microwave for an on-the-spot, nutrition-conscious, vegan-friendly meal.

INGREDIENTS:

1 15-ounce can of chickpeas, drained

$1/8$ cup of Bragg Liquid Aminos (or soy sauce)

$1/8$ cup of apple cider vinegar

4 heaping tablespoons of nutritional yeast flakes

$3/4$ teaspoon of ground cumin

$3/4$ teaspoon of garlic powder

1 tablespoon of vegetarian Worcestershire sauce (optional)

A pinch of paprika

Black pepper, to taste

DIRECTIONS:

1. Place all ingredients in a medium-sized, microwave-safe bowl. Microwave for 1 minute to soften chickpeas.

2. With a dinner fork, press the ingredients together until most of the chickpeas are broken apart. Microwave for an additional minute.

3. Stir well and enjoy as is, or try this with toast with fake mayo on it. Or, if you have time to cook brown rice, combine 2 cups of cooked rice and double all the ingredients other than the chickpeas.

This rice/chickpea combo also makes a great stuffing for red bell peppers—they should be baked at 375°F for 20 minutes.

Serves 1–2.

from Chris Saligoe

TOFU POTPIE

Chris Saligoe, who goes by "Sal," has a full plate playing guitar for the freaky and frantic Rapider Than Horsepower, playing bass for hardcore-leaning Racebannon, and cooking at the prepared foods section at his local health food grocer, where this potpie has a lot of fans. "Some lady gave me hell when she came to Bloomingfoods kinda late one night and discovered that we had run out of this dish already, since it was on the menu for that day," he says. This potpie is a hearty treat for vegans—the crust has a great flavor and the soy milk–based filling is surprisingly creamy, but when my meat-loving friend Tom sampled it, he uneasily moved the chunks of tofu around on his plate. "You know what would make this really good?" he asked. "Some chicken, or maybe some turkey!" If tofu isn't your thing, you can substitute a pound of precooked meat, either shredded or cut into chunks. And don't be discouraged by the long ingredients list—this comes together easily.

SAVORY CRUST

INGREDIENTS:

2 1/4 cups all-purpose flour

1/4 cup sucanat (this is natural sugar, but you can use brown sugar instead)

1/2 teaspoon thyme

1/2 teaspoon basil

1/2 teaspoon salt

1/2 cup canola oil

1/2 cup plain soy milk

FILLING

INGREDIENTS:

1 potato, chopped bite-sized, either scrubbed or peeled

1 small onion, diced

1 cup chopped carrot, peeled

1/4 cup olive oil

1 1/2 tespoons thyme

1 teaspoon marjoram

1 teaspoon rosemary

1 1/2 teaspoons sage

1 tablespoon salt

1 teaspoon pepper
1 1/2 cups frozen green beans
1 1/2 cups frozen corn
1 1/2 cups frozen peas
1 package of firm tofu

2 tablespoons tamari (soy sauce)
2/3 cup margarine
2/3 cup flour
2 cups plain soy milk
1/2 cup water

DIRECTIONS:

1. preheat oven to 375°F.

2. prepare crust first. whisk flour, sucanat (or brown sugar), spices, and salt in a mixing bowl. drizzle the oil into the dry ingredients, covering as much surface area as possible. mix lightly with a spatula or clean hands until you have a crumbly mixture that looks like little marbles or pebbles. drizzle in soy milk and knead into a firm dough ball. wrap in plastic and refrigerate for 30 minutes.

3. while dough is chilling, boil potato until near-soft. sauté onion, carrot, and spices in oil until onions are soft and clear. add the frozen vegetables and cook until just tender but still crisp. add potatoes, tofu, and tamari. set aside.

4. in separate small pan, make a roux by melting the margarine, then whisking in the flour, a little at a time. add the soy milk and water and whisk until smooth. let this sauce thicken for a couple minutes, whisking so it doesn't stick. add sauce to the vegetable mixture and stir. pour the veggie-tofu mixture into a large (9" x 13") oiled baking pan, filling half full.

5. unwrap dough and roll out to desired shape on a floured surface. if you don't have a rolling pin handy, a wine or beer bottle should suffice. top the filling with the crust (brush with olive oil if desired) and bake for about 15–20 minutes or until lightly browned. ta-daa!

Serves 6–8.

from Elizabeth Elmore

ASIAN STIR-FRY FOR VEGETARIANS
WHO HATE VEGETABLES

It's sad, but true—there are people who've gone vegetarian for one reason or another, but actually despise the taste and texture of vegetables. Elizabeth Elmore, front woman for Chicago's power pop four-piece the Reputation, is a member of this unlucky camp. She can barely stomach a handful of bean sprouts, but she knows that a carb-heavy diet is neither satisfying nor healthy—especially for members of touring bands. Elizabeth throws her fellow vegetable-hating vegetarians a (meat-free) bone with this simple stir-fry that she regularly enjoys on tour. "I love to cook and I actually bring a full mini kitchen with me on the road," she says. "That way I can cook real food and save money."

INGREDIENTS:

1/2 to 3/4 cup brown rice

nonstick cooking spray

1/4–1/2 cup egg substitute (vegan or the low-cal stuff)

1 teaspoon soy sauce, or more, to taste

1/2–1 teaspoon chili-garlic sauce ("Hot Cock" sauce, or if you can get it, Sambal Oelek ground chili paste, both available in most Asian grocery stores)

a shake of garlic powder

a shake of crushed chili pepper

a shake or two of black pepper

1 teaspoon sugar

1 small clove garlic, chopped very finely

1/4 small white or yellow onion, chopped very finely

1–2 teaspoons fresh ginger, chopped very finely

1 thai or serrano chili, chopped very finely

1 veggie burger (MorningStar Farms Grillers Original—not Prime—work the best by far)

dash or two of cinnamon

juice of 1/2 medium lime (or one small lime)

sweet-and-sour sauce (optional) *or* canned pineapple with juice, a pinch of brown sugar, and a pinch of cornstarch (also optional)

These instructions are pretty vague because I make this differently every time. There's definitely no need for extra salt or oil. (This is pretty healthy and low-calorie, though high in salt content.)

1. Cook the brown rice according to whatever instructions are on the box. Coat a separate pan with nonstick cooking spray and scramble the egg substitute over medium-low heat. Add some soy sauce, chili-garlic sauce, a shake of garlic powder, a shake of chili pepper, and some regular black pepper. When the egg's mostly scrambled, sprinkle sugar over the top and then scramble a couple more minutes. (For some reason, I like mine a little overcooked and chewier.) Mix into rice.

2. Clean your frying pan or coat another one with some nonstick spray, and sauté the garlic, onion, ginger, and chili. (They don't have to be chopped finely unless you don't like vegetables—by mincing them, you get the taste without the texture). When they're mostly done, add the veggie burger (seriously, use MorningStar Farms Grillers Original, they work the best) and scramble. Once scrambled, add some crushed chili pepper, regular pepper, and a dash of cinnamon. Cook some more. (It works best if the veggie burger is well cooked before you add the wet ingredients.) Then add soy sauce and chili paste to taste, and use about $1/3$ of your lime juice. Finish cooking.

3. At this point, combine the veggie burger mixture with the rice and eggs and squeeze the rest of the lime and serve, or follow one of the variations below:

   a) Mix some sweet-and-sour sauce into the final product

   or

   b) When the veggie burger is done cooking, mix in some canned pineapple, pineapple juice, and a little brown sugar into the mixture. Stir and then slowly add a little bit of cornstarch—it should thicken into a sauce.

   With either of these sauces, you can add a touch more cinnamon, if you want. You can also use MorningStar Farms Meal Starters Steak or Chik'n Strips instead of a veggie burger.

Serves 1.

from Thor Harris

THOR'S BLACK BEAN NACHOS

The first time I met Thor (née Michael) Harris, he gave me the sort of hug that most people normally reserve for long-lost friends—and I was just a girl who was making lunch for his band while they were passing through Brooklyn on tour. With broad shoulders and long, feathered hair (hence his nickname), Thor showed up on my front stoop wearing bright orange pants and a fanny pack, which, when you think about it, is a very practical accessory for somebody who's on the road. Besides being Shearwater's drummer, Thor's an accomplished carpenter who rebuilt his Austin home with such striking results that HGTV made a show about him; he's an avant garde percussionist with a couple of solo records; he's a painter; he's a really good cook; and he's one of the warmest people I've ever met. After lunch that day, Thor gave me an even bigger hug, accompanied by a promise for this nacho recipe, which his fellow band members rave about. It may seem pretty basic, but it's one of those recipes where the result is greater than the sum of its ingredients. "I eat these as a main meal almost every day when I'm at home in Austin," Thor says, "and I never get tired of them."

INGREDIENTS:

Tortilla chips

1/2 can ranch-style or black beans

2 cloves fresh garlic, chopped

1/2 lime

1/2 cup grated cheese (*asadero*, Monterey Jack, or cheddar)

1/2 cup salsa (canned or fresh)

Mesquite-flavored Bar-B-Q sauce (optional)

1 avocado (optional)

DIRECTIONS:

1. Cover a dinner plate with corn tortilla chips. Most brands are fine—On the Border makes pretty good ones that are widely available. In Austin, I usually get mine fresh from El Milagro Tortilleria.

2. Cover the chips with 1/2 can (not drained) of whole black beans (Bush's are good, or any "ranch style" black beans).

3. Sprinkle 2 chopped cloves of garlic over the beans.

4. Squeeze 1/2 a lime over that.

5. Cover the chips and beans with about 1/2 cup of grated *asadero*, cheddar, or Monterey Jack cheese.

6. Then pour about 1/2 cup of salsa over the whole thing. Canned salsas are excellent— some of my favorites are Herdez, El Pato, and Farron's. In Texas, we have about a million great salsas in jars, but if you live somewhere else, Mrs. Renfro's is pretty good.

7. (Optional) Pour 1/2 cup of mesquite-flavored BBQ sauce (any brand, but preferably not too sweet) over that.

8. Microwave the plate for 3–5 minutes, until the cheese is melted and the bottom of the plate is warm.

9. Top with avocado slices (optional) and serve immediately. You'll need a fork.

For best results, enjoy your nachos on a front porch in the late afternoon with a glass of cold Belgian ale (Kwak is my all-time favorite).

Serves 1 very hungry person or 2 moderately hungry people.

from Laura Ballance

"THAI" GRILLED MARINATED TOFU

As cofounder of Merge Records and a founding member of Superchunk, Laura Ballance is an indie rock hero—and she's also one of the coolest moms around. Let me set up a scene for you: Outside Austin's beloved BBQ joint, Pok-e-Jo's Smokehouse, Merge and Sub Pop joined forces for their 2006 SXSW day party in a field beside the restaurant. In between performances, as fans sat in the grass and sipped free Shiner Bock, a giggling little girl in stylishly mismatched clothes scampered through the crowd, trailed by a petite woman in a similar outfit. It was Laura, who then scooped up her daughter and danced toward the stage as Robert Pollard surfaced over the crowd, raising his glass and kicking in time with the first guitar chord. How rad is that? Anyway, Laura can cook, too. Drop the fish sauce if you're a strict vegetarian—or, if you're a strict carnivore, use the marinade on pork.

"This marinade is good with just about anything really. Try it with fish, shrimp, pork, or chicken."

—LAURA BALLANCE

INGREDIENTS:

3 hot serrano peppers or bird's eye
    peppers
one 6-inch stalk lemon grass cut into
    1/2-inch pieces
juice of one lime
3 tablespoons Thai fish sauce (Squid
    Brand is good, or use soy sauce if
    you're vegan)

1 tablespoon water
1/4 cup chopped fresh cilantro and/or
    basil or Thai basil
3 cloves of garlic, peeled and coarsely
    chopped
1 block firm tofu

1. Combine all ingredients except the tofu. I do it in a blender until it's pretty well pureed. If you need more liquid, pour in more fish sauce. It's smelly, but don't be afraid! Also, I vary from this according to what I have in the house. If I don't have cilantro then parsley, basil, or Thai basil will do great. Other kinds of hot peppers are fine.

2. It helps if you squeeze the tofu out before you marinate it. I set a block in a colander and set some heavy stuff on top for 15 minutes or so. Then slice up the tofu in thick slices. About 1/2 inch for grilling. Let it set in the marinade overnight in the fridge if you can. If you are not planning ahead so much, an hour will do.

3. Then grill it till it looks good to you over a moderately hot grill. Or sauté it with some stir-fry.

4. Serve with rice and a Thai-style cucumber salad.

Serves 2–3.

from Dave Lerner

SEMI-RAW EVERYDAY PASTA

Ted Leo is known for his brainy, political lyrics, but clearly, he's not the only deep thinker in his band. When it comes to raw food, Ted lets bassist Dave Lerner do the talking. It's always fun to hear from band members who don't usually get much vocal time at the mic, and Dave's treatise on raw food is funny and fascinating. If you've seen the Pharmacists play live, you know Dave as the near-motionless bass player who keeps the beat with his huge mop of hair. Like his cool and controlled stage presence, this pasta proves that he's a master of moderation. If you're not a vegan, go ahead and add the optional cheese.

"After returning home from a tour spanning most of March 2006, I decided it was detox time. This meant no alcohol, caffeine, cigarettes, or dairy products for at least two weeks. I prepared by doing some research on how to most effectively detoxify the liver, and many physicians, albeit with their typical caveats, advocate some kind of raw foods regimen in conjunction with a juice fast to assist the body's cleansing process.

"Now I'm a fairly health-conscious vegetarian, but my experience with a strictly raw diet at this point had been limited to a few meals at leading raw foods restaurants in New York City. I remember having felt great afterward, but never had the desire to take it any further. I thought about this and realized two things were holding me back from diving headlong into the world of raw food, and they were not, as many skeptics cite, time and money.

"The first glaring impediment keeping me from embracing a raw food diet was my irritation with the discourse surrounding the 'lifestyle.' At their most extreme, raw foodists tend to write about their choice of what to eat (which is, let's face it, in the grand scheme of things, a mostly functional and quotidian set of daily decisions) in terms that range from the pseudo-scientific to the out-and-out cultish. I suppose when you're dealing with life energies and limitlessly complex enzymatic reactions, it's only natural to jump from the limit of one's scientific understanding to a kind of quasi-religious wonder and its concomitant devotional and evangelical fervor. Either way, I found the countless references to 'getting the glow' and striving to be '100 percent raw' insipid. Creepier still, I'd often read claims that a raw food diet is somehow 'sexy' or can give you an 'edge on the competition.' Dubious, indeed. Still, there must be something positive to the diet if so many people testify so strongly on its behalf. So what if one side effect is the tendency to slip into objectionable prose? Could I not ignore my critical side and press on to the actual foodstuff and methods of preparation involved?

"When all is said and done, I must admit that my biggest difficulty with a totally raw diet is that it impinges on my belief that the perfect default meal is pasta, salad, and wine. I could have that most nights a week and not be too bothered. Eating raw would mean salad, sure; wine, maybe (depending on who you ask); but definitely no pasta. So I reached a compromise: keep the pasta, but make the sauce raw. This '75 percent raw solution' seemed like something I could live with.

"The following is a favorite raw pasta sauce recipe, a simple unblended pesto, adaptable to a wide range of ingredients, depending on what's at hand."

—DAVE LERNER

INGREDIENTS:

a big pinch of sea salt

4 tablespoons extra-virgin olive oil (plus a bit more)

1–2 tablespoons freshly squeezed lemon juice

1 jalapeño pepper, minced

4 cloves garlic, crushed

a bunch of basil or arugula leaves, torn into small pieces by hand. Other bitter greens like dandelion work also, as would cilantro or parsley.

$^1/_3$ cup nuts. Traditionalists favor pine nuts. Raw purists use almonds, soaked overnight and coarsely chopped. Walnuts are fine too, and have the added benefit of essential fatty acids.

$^1/_2$ box rigatoni or linguini *fina*. Any brand will do. I use Barilla.

more salt and freshly ground pepper

freshly grated cheese (optional)

DIRECTIONS:

1. Boil lots of water and don't be stingy when you add your sea salt to it.

2. In a large bowl, combine oil, lemon juice, jalapeño, crushed garlic, torn greens, and nuts. Stir aggressively with a wooden spoon until all is well combined.

3. Cook pasta, making sure not to overcook.
4. Drain pasta. Don't bother with a colander, and don't rinse it, either. Retain a small amount of cooking water, add a bit of oil, and stir. Let it cool in saucepan until it's slightly warmer than room temperature.
5. Combine pasta with sauce in your large bowl.
6. Add salt, more lemon, and freshly ground pepper, to taste.
7. If you choose, add freshly grated cheese. Raw milk cheeses are another gray area for raw foodists. I say if you're going to have cheese, go with a decent domestic Parmesan. It tastes fine, is much easier to come by than its raw counterparts, and quite a bit cheaper.
8. Serve with a sturdy, inexpensive red such as a Salice Salentino or Mas de Gourgonnier.

By the way, I fully recommend eating raw as often as possible to anyone interested. It forces creativity in cooking, and makes you more inclined to sample fruits, nuts, seeds and vegetables you might not have otherwise. Just read up and be smart about it. It's only food, but it can make you feel slightly more energized and clear once you strike the right balance. Enjoy!

Serves 2, with a bit left over.

from Matt Simon

PEANUTTY BLACK-BEAN TOFU

Part Brit-pop, part bubblegum, Austin's bouncy pop quintet Voxtrot is a very energetic band. You'll need to turn up your kitchen stereo and channel some of their exuberance before you attempt drummer Matt Simon's wild ride of a recipe. This requires one large skillet, two pots, and one bowl, so make sure you've got clean ones on hand before you start. Be sure to chop up the onion, garlic, and jalapeño in advance, too, because once you get started, you'll have to focus on three burners at once. Matt's method involves cooking the tofu slowly in oil at medium heat, which yields dense, chewy tofu. If you prefer your tofu crisp on the outside and soft on the inside, find a kitchen assistant who can keep a close eye on it and cook it on very high heat, turning frequently, while you manage the rest of the recipe.

"I came up with this recipe after I returned, absolutely broke, from tour this past December. I stared blankly at the fridge, craving something hearty and nutritious after all the potato chips and Taco Bell consumed on the way back from New York. My options were very limited: some tofu, dangerously near its expiration date, and a can of black beans in the pantry. I remembered ordering black bean tofu at a Chinese restaurant once and thinking that, even with my limited culinary skills, I could do it better. In the absence of any real alternatives, I gave it a shot, and the results were surprisingly good."

—MATT SIMON

INGREDIENTS:

1 pound firm or extra-firm tofu

1/2 cup vegetable oil

2 cups short-grain brown rice

One 15-ounce can black beans

1/4 yellow onion, chopped

2 cloves garlic, chopped

1 jalapeño, chopped

1 teaspoon thyme

3 tablespoons creamy peanut butter (or
 crunchy, if you're adventurous)
1/2 cup rice vinegar
1 tablespoon soy sauce (or to taste)
1/2 cup honey (or to taste)

black pepper to taste
3 handfuls of baby spinach (wash it first—
 nobody likes sandy spinach!)
sesame seeds (for garnish)

DIRECTIONS:

1. Put 3 1/2 cups of water in a medium-sized pot over high heat. While you're waiting for the water to come to a boil, drain and press the water from the tofu and cut it to your desired size—just not so small that it is hard to fry without it breaking up.
2. Heat the oil in a large skillet on medium heat and add the tofu.
3. When the water comes to a boil, add the brown rice, reduce to a simmer, and cover. When the oil heats up, add the tofu to the skillet.
4. Now open the black beans and drain about a quarter of the liquid from the can. Put them in a separate pot with the onion, garlic, jalapeño, and thyme and cook on low heat, stirring occasionally.
5. Make sure you are checking the tofu, and flip it when the first side is turning brown, after about 10–15 minutes. You might want to stir the rice at this point, too. Next, mix the peanut butter, rice vinegar, soy sauce, honey, and black pepper in a separate mixing bowl, until it reaches a smooth consistency.
6. Once the tofu is brown on both sides and the beans have been cooking for about 20 minutes, drain any excess oil from the tofu skillet and pour the beans over the tofu, reducing the heat to low. Next, add the peanut sauce, a little at a time, mixing the whole concoction together until it reaches the desired consistency. If there is any left over, you can serve it on the side.
7. Now put the spinach on top of the tofu and cover. Check to see if the rice is done, and turn off the heat when all the water is absorbed. Once the spinach is wilted, you are ready to serve! Serve over rice with sesame seeds sprinkled on top.

Serves 3–4.

DRINKS | SIX

WHEN IT COMES to drink recipes, I like to stick to the classics. I love an Old-Fashioned, a Tom Collins, or a Sidecar—drinks that enhance the flavor of high-quality liquor and are meant to be sipped and savored. I'm not one to shotgun beers or throw down shots with suggestive titles. I've always tried to stay away from booze masked by artificial fruit flavors, but my first taste of the John Glenn from Swearing at Motorists erased all traces of my cocktail snobbery. I hate to say it, but I think vodka and Tang were meant to be together. I also was pretty amazed by the vodka-spiked sangria from Molly Neuman, formerly of Bratmobile. Traditionally, sangria is made with brandy, and I couldn't imagine it any other way, but once you soak a bunch of fruit in a pitcher of wine for a day or two, the few shots of liquor just melt into the sweetness, so it's fine to use whatever you've got on hand.

Of course, there are a few drinks in this chapter that are even more, um, experimental—such as the Early Day Miners' Karate Kid (sake + root beer), Vague Angels' Vegan Sky Juice (soy milk + coconut rum + a whole lot more), and the Forms' Camiloflage (which, true to its title, is actually greenish-brown). Other recipe contributors add a personal touch to well-known cocktails—Irving's festive Dirty Snowflake will please adventurous White Russian fans, and They Might Be Giants fortify the Cosmo with their antioxidant-rich Countrypolitan.

For those who prefer to stick to good old-fashioned drink recipes, Nada Surf offers a traditional mojito—so traditional, in fact, that it involves a trip to Cuba, and Laura Minor shines the spotlight on one of my very favorite cocktails, the Dark 'n' Stormy. You can order this one at bars, but unless your local hangout stocks fresh ginger beer, you're better off making it at home. As a bonus, Laura also shares the one non-alcoholic beverage in this chapter—Florida East Coast Champion Sweet Tea. It's cool comfort in a glass and liquid proof that you don't have to get drunk *all* the time.

from Molly Neuman

PARTY AT YOUR OWN RISK SANGRIA

Many musicians forgo a career to pursue their artistic endeavors, but Molly Neuman has managed to make a career out of the music she loves. As drummer in the punk trio Bratmobile in the '90s, Molly helped incite the Riot Grrrl movement. She started working as a publicist for Lookout! Records and worked her way up the ranks to become a co-owner of the company. Plus, she's cofounder of an artist management company called Indivision Management Inc., and recently founded her own label, Simple Social Graces Discos. Molly is also responsible for this sangria recipe, which can be adjusted to accommodate the wildness of your party. It's best if you make it a day or two before serving, so the fruit really has time to macerate and sweeten the wine.

INGREDIENTS:

One orange

One pear

One peach

Two shots of vodka (more if you really
    want to party)

One shot of vermouth (not essential)

One bottle cheap Spanish red wine

About 2 cups of lemon soda (Sprite, 7UP,
    etc.)

DIRECTIONS:

1. Chop the fruit into cubes, put at the bottom of your pitcher.
2. Add vodka, vermouth, and red wine.
3. Let sit overnight (optional).
4. Fill to top with lemon soda.
5. Stir with wooden spoon.
6. Pour over ice into wine glasses.

Makes 1 pitcher.

from Jonathan Richardson

THE KARATE KID

Jonathan Richardson, known to friends as "Jonny Yuma," plays bass in Bloomington, Indiana's ghostly post-rock collective, Early Day Miners. He's also a publicist for Secretly Canadian, but unlike many indie rock publicists—petite, wildly enthusiastic, fast-talking girls with adorable wardrobes and perfectly uneven bangs—Jonny is a chill Midwestern guy with a giant beard. He'll never give you the hard sell, even when it comes to this original cocktail. "I've made it at parties and it's about half and half as far as drinkability," Jonathan admits. "If anything, the recipe will get people talking whether they like it or not!"

> "I drink more than I eat. My latest concoction is equal parts sake and root beer, served over ice in a tall glass. I call it the Karate Kid!!"
>
> —JONATHAN RICHARDSON

INGREDIENTS:

ice

sake

root beer

DIRECTIONS:

add ice cubes to glass. fill halfway with sake. top off with root beer. *chop chop.*

Makes 1 drink.

from Alex Tween

CAMILOFLAGE

Ecco Teres is a pseudonym kept in memory of a friend who once used it as a pen name, but many know the tall, soft-spoken singer of the Forms and founder of the label Threespheres as Alex Tween. Onstage, he is flanked by a pair of identical twins, Jackson and Brendan Kenny, who play bass and guitar respectively, and sometimes seem like they're trying to out-dance each other. The Forms don't play dance music, per se, but their short, dynamic compositions are buoyant enough to move a crowd. This recipe isn't quite as elegant as the Forms' meticulous recordings—it's more like a potent, late-night science experiment—but it really doesn't taste as bad as it sounds. I once asked Alex to make it for a potluck at my house, but he kindly replied, "I don't know if I should make Camiloflages for people . . . I don't want everyone at your party to start throwing up."

"the camiloflage gets its name from its greenish-black color as well as from a writer named camilo who reviewed a bootleg copy of our 1st album for pitchfork years before it came out." —ALEX TWEEN

INGREDIENTS:

2 parts Midori melon

1/4 part o.j.

1 part Coke

DIRECTIONS:

yes, Coke. upon seeing the black liquid swirling and not quite blending within the green, most are sickened. but just about everyone who has been forced to try the camiloflage has begrudgingly admitted they thought it was ok.

pour ingredients into a glass without stirring them together, and then start diluting the camiloflage using:

ice

tonic or seltzer, or *Diet* Sprite! the one and only context where Diet Sprite is actually not that bad.

don't stir anything. the heterogeneous mix of liquids is part of the camiloflage's charm, similar to the scrolling oil blobs theaters would show before the start of the movie. also, be warned, the camiloflage is stronger than you think. *salud.*

Makes 1 drink.

from Steven Scott

DIRTY SNOWFLAKE

At an end-of-tour show at Emo's in Austin, hometown favorites Voxtrot and Los Angeles' Irving brought down the house with a double-shot of power pop. With their peppy, '60s-inspired tunes, Irving sounds something like a modern-day Monkees. My roommate, Shannon (who, conveniently enough, is also my literary agent) was vacationing in Austin at the time and scored this recipe from their bass player, Steven Scott. If you're into White Russians, give this creamy and minty coffee-flavored cocktail a try.

"this is a wintery evening drink . . . a great drink to trim the tree with . . ."   —STEVEN SCOTT

start with a full glass of ice. then add:

1 part vodka (skye or absolut)
1 part kahlúa (or other coffee liquor. but
   kahlúa is best)

¹/2 part peppermint schnapps

fill remainder with half and half or whole milk or combination.
mix well (shaken in martini shaker is best . . .)
garnish with fresh ground cinnamon and fresh ground nutmeg (leave on top, or mix it in
   a little . . . it's best to provide scent, not necessarily for flavor)
that's it!! light a fire and drink a few.

Makes 1 drink.

from Laura herself

DARK 'N' STORMY FLORIDA &
FLORIDA EAST COAST CHAMPION SWEET TEA

If Patsy Cline were to be reborn into the Gainesville, Florida, punk rock scene, she might have ended up sounding like Laura Minor. I get goose bumps every time I hear Laura sing—her voice is strong and sweet, like whiskey and roses. Her country ballads ride heavy dub grooves, and her lyrics reach out to the bad girls in the house. In my favorite song of hers, she croons about being too drunk to climb into bed, and begs for two cool pillows to place between the floor and her head. Laura considers herself a foodie, but doesn't do a lot of cooking, so she's sharing a pair of drinks recipes—the first is a fantastic cocktail that's hard to find in bars, and the second compensates for its lack of booze with an inordinate amount of sugar.

DARK 'N' STORMY FLORIDA

"I discovered this drink during the brutal summer months in Gainesville, Florida, and into the hurricane season. If you have ever supplemented your income as a musician with bartending, you might have come across this amazing drink.

"But if you haven't . . .

"Dark 'N' Stormy is the national drink of Bermuda. Discard all cultural, social stereotypes of rum drinks and enjoy this spicy beverage in hot or cold weather. Serve with percussion instruments."

—LAURA MINOR

INGREDIENTS:

2 ounces dark rum (I recommend really good Haitian rum, like Rhum Barbancourt 15-year or 4-year)

4 ounces ginger beer (you can find homemade ginger beer at most Caribbean restaurants). Do not use ginger ale.

a pinch of sugar

1. Build in a Collins glass; stir with cracked ice.
2. Garnish with any or all of these items:

*slices of fresh ginger	*a sprinkling of nutmeg
*a squeeze of lemon (most recipes call for lime, but I like lemon)	*a squeeze of lime
	*a sprig of mint

If you are traveling through a college town in the summer, be sure to pour an entire bottle of this spicy drink into a juicy watermelon and, after the show, share with your friends in the nearest backyard. Do not use a machete to cut open the watermelon.

Makes 1 drink.

FLORIDA EAST COAST CHAMPION SWEET TEA

INGREDIENTS:	EQUIPMENT:
3 family-sized Tetley tea bags	wooden spoon
1 to 1 1/3 cups of sugar	glass saucepan with lid
(Some people add a tiny pinch of baking soda to reduce any bitterness.)	

DIRECTIONS:

1. In saucepan, bring 3–4 cups of water, the sugar, and the optional pinch of baking soda to a boil and stir with wooden spoon.
2. Add 3 family-sized tea bags (or 5–6 small tea bags) and reduce heat to a simmer for about 1 minute.
3. Do not "boil" the tea; it will inevitably turn out bitter and cloudy and break your heart in two. Remove from heat and cover. Allow to sit for at least 10–15 minutes, then remove tea bags.
4. Pour into gallon pitcher and fill with ice cubes and cold water. Refrigerate.

I prefer Tetley, but some go with Luzianne. Tetley is undoubtedly smoother. This beverage is highly addictive. Your doctor may try to reduce your intake to one pot a day and you will inevitably start lying and hiding tea bags around the house. Serve with a pillow and good conversation. Enjoy!!

Makes a gallon of tea.

from Daniel Lorca

PATRIOT ACT *MOJITOS*

In terms of duration and brightness, Nada Surf's lush, gleaming pop songs are like sparklers—they burn like there's no tomorrow and never last as long as you wish they would. If all you've heard from this Brooklyn trio is their 1996 radio hit, "Popular," then you've got some serious catching up to do. Start by downloading "The Blankest Year" (get the version with explicit lyrics, if possible), and enjoy two minutes twelve seconds of pure triumph. Follow with a *mojito*, courtesy of bass player Daniel Lorca.

> "Leave the USA. Purchase some Havana Club rum and try not to get arrested this time when you bring it back into the country, you might end up, irony of ironies, in Guantanamo with a plastic bag over your head. If you make this with anything other than real rum from Cuba, you are wasting your time."
>
> —DANIEL LORCA

INGREDIENTS:

bunch of fresh mint

tablespoon of sugar

lemon

ice

Cuban rum

sparkling water

DIRECTIONS:

1. In a highball, crush a good amount of mint and about a tablespoon of sugar, then add the juice of a lemon.
2. Fill the glass with ice, add rum to about two thirds of the way up, top with fizzy mineral water, and give it a brief stir.

Makes 1 drink.

from David Doughman

THE JOHN GLENN

There are only two people in Swearing at Motorists, so it's fortunate that singer/guitarist Dave Doughman has more combustible energy than the average three bands rolled together. His voice is big and bold, and his performances involve a great deal of jumping, kicking, and iconic rock poses. He's a character offstage, too. When I asked him to sign a cookbook-related document at a day party at Austin's Club de Ville, he backed away dramatically and claimed to have a phobia of blue pens. He proceeded to ask strangers around the bar for a black pen, and then happily signed the form—along with a lengthy autograph-style note to me, and offered to share the vat of John Glenns he had waiting in his van. Having already tried the John Glenn at home, I knew it was too early in the day for me to get into that kind of trouble. Be very careful with this one—it'll knock you out.

INGREDIENTS:

Tang instant breakfast drink

Absolut Vodka (or your favorite brand, or whatever you can get with those drink tickets)

DIRECTIONS:

1. Follow directions on Tang to make a pitcher of the astronaut's favorite elixir.
2. Depending on the desired taste and effects pour vodka into a glass until 25–50 percent full, then finish filling the glass with Tang, shake or pour, then enjoy.

   For a "Buzz Aldrin," substitute Jack Daniel's for vodka.

Makes 1 drink at a time,
but watch out because you're gonna want more.

from John Flansburgh

THE COUNTRYPOLITAN

Most bands choose between quantity and quality. They Might Be Giants chooses both. Named for one of my favorite movies, this Brooklyn duo comprises one of the world's most distinctive and prolific bands. After playing together for over a quarter of a century and writing literally hundreds of songs, John Linnell and John Flansburgh continue to straddle genres and keep things funny and interesting. Their cocktail here is exceptionally refined, pleasantly tart, and packed with antioxidants, thanks to its natural cranberry-and-pomegranate-juice combo. It's quite strong, too. My mom loves this one, but since she's a lightweight, she likes to drink one part Countrypolitan with three parts seltzer.

"Developed deep in the Catskill Mountains of New York State by city folk for city folk; this is a variation on the Cosmopolitan, the cocktail of highly effective drinkers. Real cranberry juice can be found at your local health food store. While it is far more acidic, the sweetness of the pomegranate juice will equalize things, while providing another dimension in flavor."   —JOHN FLANSBURGH

INGREDIENTS:

2 parts vodka (not infused)

1 part Cointreau

1 part real cranberry juice (not cranberry juice cocktail)

1 part pomegranate juice

A liberal amount of fresh lime juice

DIRECTIONS:

1. Shake with ice, and strain into a martini or champagne cocktail glass.

Makes 1 drink,
or increase quantities to make a whole pitcher.

from Chris Leo

VEGAN SKY JUICE

Chris Leo was formerly the front man of Native Nod, the Van Pelt, and the Lapse, and now leads Vague Angels with his eerie, singsongy spoken-word lyrics. His powerful coconut-scented cocktail is a lot of fun to read about, and if you like his writing style, you should check out *White Pigeons*, his novel about a starving musician. Fictitious as it may be, chapter seven is a CD from the band in the book—and members of Vague Angels play the characters' parts. Chris is a member of the very talented Leo clan from Bloomfield, New Jersey—his brothers are Ted Leo (of the Pharmacists) and Danny Leo (of the Holy Childhood).

"I'm not much of a cook, but I was a finalist in 2001's Grand Marnier cocktail competition. I'm obsessed with gin, but the strong botanicals make it a difficult booze to mix. Back in the day, I thought Grand Marnier, pineapple, and Sprite were the best ingredients to hook the non–gin drinkers on gin, but on vacation with my girlfriend in the Bahamas this past winter I found another: Sky Juice. Here's my vegan take on it.

"Sky Juice is the Bahamian version of the piña colada. Now, drinking rum under the oppressive Caribbean sun may waft one's worries away on a sargassum zephyr, but the addition of gin to the mix will instigate the mind to further take matters into one's own hands by removing one's shirt and convincing others around one to do the same. Bahamian women fear the husband who returns after a dinner of conch and Sky Juice. 'Children from the Sky' isn't necessarily as poetic as it sounds. This version is vegan for both the ethical and un-.

"Traditionally, Sky Juice gets its cream from a combination of coconut milk and condensed cow milk. By replacing those with vanilla soy milk, it not only becomes less fatty, but you also replace the dairy-induced phlegm with estrogen-related isoflavones, thereby increasing the drink's already high aphrodisiacal effects.

"I've also chosen to sweeten it with Equal because, let's face it, drinkers, diabetes will kill us long before cancer unless we learn to balance our vices—get used to Equal.

> "And finally, cinnamon brings out the vanilla, jumpstarts the metabolism, and helps process sugar. Get it on."
>
> —CHRIS LEO

INGREDIENTS:

3 counts of gin

2 counts of coconut rum (Malibu, Captain Morgon Parrot Bay, etc.)

1 packet of Equal

2 big dashes of cinnamon

2 counts of vanilla soy milk

ice

DIRECTIONS:

1. Blend it or shake it hard.
2. Garnish with a beach.

Serves 1.

DESSERTS | SEVEN

WHEREVER YOU MAY find yourself, a simple dessert can bring you home. When I was feeling homesick in college, a thick, buttered slice of my mom's Irish soda bread was the one thing that could transport me back to our Long Island kitchen, where the round oak table would be set with paper plates and coffee mugs of steaming tea. It can get lonely on the road, but Syd Butler of Les Savy Fav finds the same taste of home in his mom's Butterscotch Pie, and John Vanderslice finds it in his mother's one-dish Fresh-Fruit Cobbler. It's Banana Pudding that brings Patterson Hood from the Drive-By Truckers back to his Grandma Sissy's house, and Strawberry Pop Cake that sends Catfish Haven's George Hunter back to his childhood birthday parties. These time-tested recipes have already gotten a lot of mileage in my kitchen, and I hope they'll help you make some new memories in yours.

from Liz and Ben Kweller

CHOCOLATE BALLS

The first time I met Ben Kweller, he was opening for Lemonheads' lead man Evan Dando at an Eastern Long Island club called the Stephen Talkhouse, where it feels like you're watching a show in somebody's living room. With a harmonica strapped to his head like a night-brace and an acoustic guitar that seemed to be twice his size, BK ran from corner to corner of the empty stage as he played, looking sort of like a hyperactive child—he was barely twenty at the time. At first we giggled, but then we cheered. If I wrote songs as catchy as his, I think I'd be running all over the place, too. BK plays much bigger rooms nowadays, and he's got a band to keep him company and block his stage-long sprints. This recipe is a joint effort from BK and his lovely wife, Liz.

"If it's a delicious and addictive dessert you're looking for, nothing compares to these famous Chocolate Balls. There is no baking required. It's a super easy recipe, but the final product seems very complex and leaves your friends enamored. These balls are great for holidays, parties or just for snacking around the house."

—BEN KWELLER

INGREDIENTS:

1 cup finely ground walnuts or pecans

2 1/2 cups crushed vanilla wafers

One 6-ounce bag chocolate chips

1/2 cup granulated sugar

3 tablespoons corn syrup

1/2 cup orange juice

DIRECTIONS:

1. Use food processor to grind nuts and wafers.
2. Melt chocolate chips over low heat.
3. Stir in sugar and corn syrup until sugar dissolves.
4. Add orange juice.

5. Remove from heat and stir in wafers and nuts until dough is formed.
6. Chill dough in refrigerator.
7. Roll dough into balls 1" in diameter.
8. Roll balls around in granulated sugar.
9. Place balls in a tin to store. Chocolate Balls taste best after they ripen in the fridge for 2–3 days.

Makes 2 to 3 dozen balls.

from George's mom, María Hunter

STRAWBERRY POP CAKE

In his earliest performances, a young, nervous Otis Redding would race through his songs at breakneck speed and send his backing band into an unexpected frenzy, tearing at the seams and crashing on cue. Catfish Haven, a band named for the trailer park that singer George Hunter grew up in, channels that raw, soulful sound from so long ago. As their original songs imply, these guys are steeped in the classics. If you invite them over for dinner and put on some soul records, they'll sing along for hours—and when George really gets into it, you'll feel like you've got Sam Cooke in your living room. With his deep voice, long ponytail, and soft-spoken demeanor, George isn't somebody you'd immediately peg as a fan of hot-pink strawberry cake, yet he raves about this treat that his mother made for him every year on his birthday when he was growing up. Keep in mind that "strawberry pop" means "strawberry soda," and rest assured that this cake is *very* sweet—even before you fill it with Jell-O and blanket it with Cool Whip.

INGREDIENTS:

1 box of white cake mix

4 eggs

2 cans of strawberry pop (you'll need about 26 ounces total)

1 stick of melted butter

1 box of vanilla instant pudding

1 box strawberry Jell-O

1 large tub of Cool Whip

DIRECTIONS:

1. Preheat oven to 300°F.

2. Combine cake mix, 4 eggs, 1¼ cups of strawberry pop, 1 stick of melted butter, and vanilla pudding.

3. Mix on low speed for 3 minutes. Pour into a 9" x 13" cake pan, and bake for 32–36 minutes. Cake is done when toothpick inserted in center comes out clean.

3. When cake is done, poke lots of holes in the cake. Make sure fork or tool used hits bottom. Set cake aside.

FOR JELL-O:

4. In saucepan combine 1 box of strawberry Jell-O and 2 cups of strawberry pop. Place on stove top over medium heat and stir until Jell-O is dissolved.
5. Pour over holes in cake. Refrigerate for at least 1 hour.
6. Spread Cool Whip over top of cake.

Serves a sweet-toothed crowd.

from Devendra himself

AFRICANITAS RICAS

These days, anybody who pays a little attention to the music press knows who Devendra Banhart is, but when he e-mailed me this recipe a few years ago, all I knew was that he'd heard about the cookbook from our mutual friend, Thor Harris from Shearwater. When you read this recipe, you'll understand why I was intrigued enough to go out and buy a couple of his records. Now I have Thor to thank for introducing me to one of my favorite songwriters. His unusual and soothing voice is always floating from my kitchen radio, and his live shows are wild. Last time I saw Devendra in New York, his twenty-person entourage piled onto the stage with him and were dancing, singing, and making out with each other as much as the kids in the audience were. Devendra brings the party anywhere he goes, and if you're lucky, he'll bring his fried bananas, too.

RIGHT ON!!!!!!
here is my favorite recipe for:
AFRICANITAS RICAS
you shall require!

INGREDIENTS:

many bananas!
two eggggs!!
a little bit of cream!!

a box of graham crackers!!!
a big piece of butter!
SOUR CREAM!!
HONEY!

DIRECTIONS:

now, chop the beautyful godsends (the bananas) into the size of 8 quarters glued together. do this with all the beautyfulll godsends.

next, crack the eggggs and put 'em in a bowl, add a little bit of cream!! And

STIRRRRRR!!!!! leave the bowl alone and get another bowl, crush the graham crackers into a fine fine powder! liike sand!

SIR

LAWRENCE

OF ARABIA!!!!!!!!

put it in bowl number two!

now take a BIG frying pan and put a BIG piece of butter on it, but don't turn it on or nothing.

now, turn it ON! but LOW!!! real LOW! and do this!::::

dip the godsend (banana) into the egg mixture,

then dip the godsend covered in egg in the graham cracker bowl till the whole godsend is covered in a layer of the stuff,

THEN, put it on the frying pan!!!! let it get GOLDEN!!!!!!!!!! flip it over !!!!!! mmmmmmmmmmmmmmmmmmmmmm its looking sooo GGOOOD!!!!

now, have ready a plate with paper towels on it!!! put the GOLDEN godsend on the plate with the paper towel and let it cool for about 5 minutes 'cause it oughta be WARM!!!!

do this with all the godsends!!!!!!!!!!!!

NOW! transfer the warm and GOLDEN godsends to a beautyful wooden plate (preferably AFRICAN!) or fancy New Orleans looking plate with peacocks and sweet scenes painted in watercolor,

NOW! put a DAB of the sour cream, just cover the top!, of our GOLDEN godsends,

now!!! put a DAB of that sweet HONEY on the sour cream!!! and

UIGI>GIUG:IYFUYFTYDKYDKYDKYDTRDDTKMYTDYTFJ<GBK?HNLJN :LJM:MJL:?HNL?KHBKLJBK.JV.JKH.VJYHFVYJFYFCUJ,.FCJHCVJ,HCV,JGHCV J,HGCYHTDYJDTJDTRHSDT

AAAFFFRRIIIICCCAAANNNIIITTTAAASSSSSSSSSSS

RRRRRRRRIIIICCCCAAASSSSSSSS!!!!!!!!!!!!!!!!!!!!!!!!!!!!

Depending on how big they are,
each godsend will serve 1–2 people.

from Patterson Hood and Jenn Bryant

SISSY'S BANANA PUDDING

If I had to place a bet on a last-man-standing guitar solo marathon, a whiskey-drinking contest, an arm-wrestling championship, or an all-out bar brawl between the Drive-By Truckers and any other band in this book, I'd put my money on the Truckers every time. In fact, whatever the battle involved, I'd probably just warn their opponents to forfeit. The Truckers are among the toughest, tightest, and most tireless bands around, but don't let their slow Southern drawls throw you off—their sharp liberal politics are as much a part of their performances as the bottle of Jack on the stage floor. And in between thick guitar riffs, they spin stories that would make Carson McCullers and William Faulkner proud. When they sing about banana pudding in a song called "Sinkhole," it's served up after the last supper for a banker who is attempting to repossess a family farm. The farm's fifth-generation patriarch buries the banker's body and doesn't think twice about going to church the next day—and the song is one of the Truckers' most triumphant. Like I said, don't mess with these guys.

"This recipe was donated by my dear friend and our band's Web mistress, Jenn Bryant. She named the banana pudding after my beloved grandmother Sissy, who in addition to making me incredible banana pudding that tasted exactly like this recipe, also supported my old band, Adam's House Cat, by letting us practice in her basement for six years of very loud Rock and Roll without a single complaint ever. She passed away while I was touring in 2002. Every time Jenn makes me this banana pudding, the memories race through my head and for a few moments I feel like a kid again at my grandmother's house."

—PATTERSON HOOD

"Making the best real, old-fashioned banana pudding requires two things—patience and the purest ingredients you can find. I'm quite ridiculous about it—I have paid twenty dollars for a bottle of vanilla just to see if 'the good stuff' makes any difference. It did, a tiny bit, but truthfully as long as you're using REAL ingredients—real butter, whole milk, real vanilla, brand-name fresh vanilla wafers—it turns

THE BANANA PUDDING PART

INGREDIENTS:

box of vanilla wafers

4–5 ripe bananas

$^7/_8$ cup sugar

$^1/_2$ cup all-purpose flour

$^1/_2$ teaspoon salt

2 cups milk (whole)

1 teaspoon vanilla extract (not imitation)

4 egg yolks (large)

1 tablespoon butter (not margarine)

DIRECTIONS:

1. Preheat oven to 375°F.
2. Get your 9" x 9" baking dish (glass seems to work the very best, but anything will do) and put a layer of whole vanilla wafers covering the bottom. I like a bunch of wafers so if you overlap a few, that's okay.
3. Now get out your bananas. A lot of people use really ripe bananas to make banana pudding. I've had much better results with almost green bananas; the ripe ones don't have the texture and tanginess to offset the sweetness of the pudding. Peel and slice the bananas into a bowl. You should cover the banana slices with plastic wrap to keep the air from darkening them.
4. Next, mix the sugar, flour, and salt in a bowl, and stir well. Make sure there aren't any lumps in the mixture. Put this aside for a minute.
5. Mix your milk and vanilla together in a cup and place both this mixture and the sugar mixture beside the stove.
6. In a heavy saucepan, whisk the egg yolks until they are well beaten. Over medium heat, add the flour/sugar/salt mixture to the egg yolks, alternately with the milk and vanilla mixture, stirring constantly. Stirring constantly is the key to this pudding.

7. Bring to a gentle boil (but be careful not to scorch it) and, when the mixture begins to get thick, add the butter. Keep boiling and keep stirring until mixture reaches a nice pudding consistency. Remove from heat.

8. Get your bananas out and lay a layer of banana slices in the baking dish on top of the vanilla wafers; make sure they are touching, so you have a nice thick layer. Pour half of the pudding over the banana & wafer layer and spread it over evenly. Repeat the process with another layer of vanilla wafers, another layer of banana slices, and cover with the remaining pudding.

MERINGUE

INGREDIENTS:

4 egg whites, at room temperature

¹/₄ teaspoon cream of tartar

5 tablespoons sugar

¹/₂ teaspoon vanilla extract

DIRECTIONS:

The meringue is tougher. It's important that your egg whites are room temperature. Whipping them steadily and not too much is also key. If you're lucky enough to have a copper bowl, you can drop the cream of tartar from the meringue ingredients and just whip your egg whites in that; copper gives the egg whites the same thing that cream of tartar does.

1. Using a whisk or an electric hand mixer, beat the egg whites at high speed until they form soft peaks. Mix in the cream of tartar. Still mixing at high speed, gradually add the sugar, a tablespoon at a time, and beat until stiff peaks form. Fold the vanilla into the meringue.

2. When it looks good and stiff, spread the meringue over the pudding, sealing it at the sides of the dish.

3. Bake in a preheated 375°F oven until meringue browns, 12 to 15 minutes, depending upon your oven. Then, once the peaks are nice and brown, take the pudding out and

dig in! If you don't like warm banana pudding, then you can cover it with plastic wrap (I find using toothpicks to hold the wrap off the meringue keeps it looking pretty) and refrigerate until cold. This banana pudding tastes delicious both ways!

Makes 1 tray of edible heaven—
try not to eat it all by yourself.

from Alex Kapranos

LEMON GINGER FLAPJACKS

While on tour, Franz Ferdinand's lead man, Alex Kapranos, writes a column for *The Guardian* in the UK about the food he eats and the people he meets as he travels the world with his band. For music and food fans, each eloquent and witty entry is more delicious than the last—and he's compiled some of his favorite stories for a book called *Sound Bites* (Fig Tree, November 2006). When he's back home in Glasgow and cooking for himself, these flapjacks are among his favorite homemade snacks. But don't be misled—in Scotland, "flapjack" is *not* another word for "pancake." These buttery, granola bar–like treats are better served at tea-time than breakfast time, but you'll need to scope out the cereal aisle to find the oats Alex recommends using. Look for old-fashioned or steel-cut Irish oats, which are available in most well-stocked supermarkets.

"This is an easy recipe that kids could follow. Most musicians should also be able to attempt it if properly supervised. Try to get a bag of oats that haven't been rolled too much. It's best if the grains are still relatively whole—you get a better, more open texture than porridge oats, which have been chopped up a bit."

—ALEX KAPRANOS

GET THIS STUFF . . .

INGREDIENTS:

Rind of a lemon

Fresh ginger root to taste—2 inches is
    usually enough

2 parts butter (about half a cup, or one stick)

1 part sugar (about $1/4$ cup)

1 part honey (about $1/4$ cup)*

steel-cut oats (about 1 cup)

*You can use golden syrup instead of honey, margarine instead of butter, and powdered instead of fresh ginger, but what's the point? You'll save 50p and it'll taste minging.

1. Preheat oven to 350°F.

2. Grate the lemon rind and ginger.

3. Melt the butter in a pan over a low heat, then add the sugar and honey. Keep heating until the sugar has dissolved, then pour it into a mixing bowl.

4. Mix in the rind, ginger, and some oats, then stir. Keep adding oats until all the liquid has been absorbed. Enough oats should be added so that they are moist enough to stay bound together, but not too sloppy.

5. Spread the mix over a buttered baking tray. Bake for around half an hour.

You can experiment with different temperatures and timings—it's one of those simple recipes that you can have a lot of fun fiddling with. It'll probably take a couple of attempts to make them the way you like them. Instead of ginger and lemon you can use dried fruit, nuts and other spices like cinnamon. Dried apricot and walnut is pretty good, too.

Serves 4.

from Carey Mercer

CHOCOLATE WORM

You never really know what to expect from Frog Eyes. When I first met the British Columbian four-piece, we were all waking up at the cozy Austin home of our friends Dylan and Phil during SXSW. They seemed like polite, ordinary people, appreciative of the house coffee and the house cats, but later that evening, as the warm-up and backing band for Destroyer, they showed another side of themselves. Wrapped in ninja headbands, they worked the crowd into a fury with Carey Mercer's theatrical delivery and madcap lyrics. Next thing you know, they're sipping beers after the show and raving about Carey's baking skills. The fun doesn't stop. This dessert recipe/edible sculpture is perfect for Halloween, though the band enjoys it year-round.

INGREDIENTS:

A pre-made apple crisp or white cake in a
    rectangular cake pan
2–3 fresh mandarin oranges (clementines
    or tangerines work, too)

A bag of chocolate chips
2 pieces of black licorice candy

DIRECTIONS:

1. Construct in an oblong rectangular glass baking tray, through modern baking techniques, some form of firm dessert—apple crisp is nice if you wish to simulate the broken ground of a spring prairie field. One could also use one of those white cakes to create an arctic analogue—the possibilities for the worm's landscape are as plentiful as the earth itself.

2. Take 2 or 3 mandarin oranges and carefully peel them. Make sure the oranges are of a consistent size. Now carefully pull the mandarin oranges in half. Place the halved oranges onto your dessert, from top to bottom, running lengthwise, so that the halved

oranges resemble the humps of the back of a worm, rising out of the humble land that produces vital sustenance for the blessed workers.

3. In a pan, melt the finest chocolate chips that money can purchase.

4. Carefully (so as not to burn yourself or create a visual object not desired) pour the chocolate over the humps of the worm, creating a shiny chocolate skin that also allows the viewer the occasional glimpse of the worm's mandarin interior.

5. THE MOST IMPORTANT PART: Purchase 2 fine licorice candies from your local Dutch market. The licorice goodies must be circular and have a black exterior that wraps itself around a tempting orange center. Place the licorice candies on the crest of the top mandarin bump, so as to create the worm's tender eyes. Now you have a CHOCOLATE WORM who looks up at you and your company, begging for your forks and knives to dig in!

Makes 1 very decorated apple crisp or cake.

from Ed Droste's mom

PECAN PIE

Like heavily sedated woodland sprites, the three members of Grizzly Bear play forest folk that's as magical as it is mellow. In their spare compositions, breathy vocals and subtle electronic squeaks melt between clarinet tones and wind chimes. It's fitting that lead singer Ed Droste submitted this simple and homey dessert, which turns out far greater than the sum of its parts.

INGREDIENTS:

1 cup dark brown sugar

1 stick of butter

1 cup corn dark syrup (look for the Karo brand—it has a blue label)

4 eggs

1 teaspoon vanilla

1 bag of pecans

1 prepared pie shell

vanilla ice cream (optional)

DIRECTIONS:

1. take dark brown sugar and stick of butter and melt in saucepan.
2. take off heat and add 1 cup syrup.
3. in a bowl, mix four eggs with mixer or whisk if need be.
4. add to cooled butter mixture with teaspoon vanilla.
5. pour into prepared pie shell and put pecans on top.
6. bake in preheated 350°F oven until center is not all gooey—about 45 minutes.

vague instructions, i know, but that's what my mom said, and every time i make it, it's so good! i get mom to make one every time i come home. haha. so yum. needs vanilla ice cream on top.

Makes 1 pie.

from Sam Fogarino

CACAO ROSSO

If you're the drummer who provides the evil backbeat for a world-famous band named for an international espionage agency, then you probably don't want your name showing up next to a recipe for "Chocolate-Covered Strawberries with Cookies and Homemade Whipped Cream." So, thank goodness Interpol's Sam Fogarino came up with a smooth title for this treat—he gets to keep his street cred, and we get a deliciously unpretentious dessert. Along with singer Paul Banks, Sam did a lot of cooking for the band during the recording sessions for both of Interpol's records, and he loves to cook in his New York City apartment. "I live in my cubicle of a kitchen," he says. To save time, Sam picks up his chocolate *pizzelle*s (thin, wafer-like Italian cookies) at a gourmet grocery store, but if you have a *pizzelle* iron, you can make your own.

HERE'S WHAT YOU NEED:

INGREDIENTS:

approximately 32 ounces of fine quality plain chocolate—mix dark and milk to taste

6 long-stem strawberries—go for the driscoll's!

6 chocolate *pizzelle* cookies

1/2 pint of heavy whipping cream—we all know how to make whipped cream, right?*

DIRECTIONS:

1. in the bottom part of a double boiler, bring water to a soft boil. then, add the chocolate to the top part, stir constantly as it melts, and when it's fully melted, take the double-boiler off the heat.

*Well, just in case you don't: Put a metal bowl and the beater attachments from an electric mixer in the freezer for a few minutes. When they're cold, dump some chilled cream into the bowl and beat at medium speed. Add confectioners' sugar to taste, and stop mixing as soon as soft peaks form.

2. dip each strawberry in the hot melted chocolate.

3. let chill until chocolate has cooled and hardened.

4. have the whipped cream ready, and add one dollop to each chocolate *pizzelle*.

5. then, gently place each chocolate-covered berry onto the creamed *pizzelle*.

6. eat.

Makes 6 embellished chocolate-covered strawberries.

from JV's mom, Jean Young

ONE-DISH FRESH-FRUIT COBBLER

John Vanderslice, a fine singer-songwriter and owner of San Francisco's illustrious analog recording studio, Tiny Telephone, owes his recipe contribution—and his success—to a very special lady. "It's from my mom, Jean Young, a beautiful woman who allowed me to be creative and make my own way in the world." Ms. Young, in turn, gives credit to her own mother: "This recipe was perfected by my Southern-born and -raised grandmama and mama, but feel free to adjust the ingredients, particularly the butter and sugar, to your own tastes."

INGREDIENTS:

1/2 stick (four tablespoons) butter, sliced
    into squares

1 cup all-purpose flour

2 teaspoons baking powder

1/2 teaspoon salt

1/2 teaspoon freshly grated nutmeg
    (reduce to 1/4 teaspoon if using dried
    nutmeg)

2/3 cup sugar or to taste

2/3 cup milk

2 1/4 cups fresh organic blueberries or
    sliced peaches, or best of all,
    a combination of both

DIRECTIONS:

1. Preheat oven to 375°F.
2. Add butter to an 8" square or other 2-quart baking dish, and melt the butter by putting the pan in the oven for a minute.
3. Sift the flour into a bowl, along with baking powder, salt, and nutmeg, and stir in sugar until combined.
4. Add milk and whisk batter until it is just combined—do not overbeat.

5. Pour the fruit into the melted butter and the batter on top. Do not stir, but you can shake the pan to even the combination out.
6. Bake in middle of oven for about 40 minutes or until brown.
7. Serve warm with ice cream or real whipped cream.

Makes 1 fruit crisp.

from Syd's mom, Julie Butler

BUTTERSCOTCH PIE

Les Savy Fav's raucous performances are marked by singer Tim Harrington's on-stage costume changes. During a recent show at Brooklyn's Warsaw, the Polish National Home–turned–rock venue, he stripped out of a three-piece suit and into some red undies before slipping into a fur cape, then a flesh-toned catsuit with all of his organs drawn on it, Visible Man–style, then a pair of pink sweatpants with a T-shirt that read, "Please Feed This Man." Bassist Syd Butler helps Tim keep his burly figure in shape with tour-ready kitchen specialties, like this rich pie recipe. "I made it for the band once when we spent Thanksgiving in San Fran on tour," Syd says. "It's not very common, but it's so good."

INGREDIENTS:

1 cup of brown sugar, packed

1/4 teaspoon of salt

6 tablespoons of flour

2 egg yolks

2 cups of milk

2 tablespoons of butter

1/2 teaspoon of vanilla

1 ready-made pie crust

DIRECTIONS:

1. Heat 1 inch of water in the bottom half of a double boiler over medium heat, and add the brown sugar, salt, and flour to the top half. Stir slowly.

2. Beat in the egg yolks and continue to stir until completely blended. Gradually add milk and continue to stir.

3. When the mixture thickens, add the butter. Cover and cook on medium heat for 10 minutes.

4. Uncover, stir in the vanilla, and allow to cool slightly. Pour mixture into pie crust and chill the pie in the fridge for 1 hour.

Makes 1 pie.

from Correne "Guinea Love" Spero

7-LAYER BARS

Three white girls from Long Island in a hip-hop group? This sounds like another hare-brained idea from Diddy's Reality TV Think Tank, and yet, it's the story of Northern State's career. As a trio of best friends living in New York City, they named their band after the Northern State Parkway, which delivered them from their hometown of Dix Hills. Then, they renamed themselves. On stage, Robyn Goodmark goes by Sprout, Julie Potash calls herself Hesta Prynn (after the Hawthorne protagonist who was scorned for banging a Puritan minister), and Correne Spero, blessed with a tough Italian surname, just drops her first name. Their rhymes tackle pop culture and girl-power themes, and this recipe proves that feminist rappers can still whip up a mean dessert.

"These have been a Spero family standard for years. Yes, you do need to use the sweetened condensed milk, even though it's truly gross. I tried to make them without it and somebody may have cracked a filling at Hesta Prynn's holiday party due to this misstep." —CORRENE SPERO

INGREDIENTS:

1 cup butter or margarine

1 cup graham crackers, crushed

1 (6–8 ounces) package butterscotch
   chips

1 (6–8 ounces) package chocolate chips

1 cup flaked coconut

1 cup pecans, chopped

One 14-ounce can sweetened condensed
   milk

DIRECTIONS:

1. Preheat oven to 350°F.
2. Melt butter in 9" x 13" pan.
3. Sprinkle graham cracker crumbs and layer the next 4 ingredients.

4. DO NOT STIR!
5. Pour milk over all ingredients.
6. Bake at 350°F for 20–30 minutes.
7. Let it cool completely.
8. Cut into bars.

*Makes a large tray of bars—
certainly enough for a bumpin' holiday party.*

from Zach Thomas

BUTTERMILK PIE

A dessert recipe passed along from your mom or grandma can be the next best thing to a hometown-bound plane ticket, unless, of course, you don't have a kitchen-equipped home anymore. Lots of bands move out of their apartments and put their belongings in storage before heading out on tour—to avoid paying rent on the places they leave vacant. This was the situation for Okkervil River's lead man, Will Sheff, in the spring of 2004. He was feeling uneasy about being back home in Austin without his own place, and to make matters worse, his car had recently been laid to rest. Bassist and mandolin player Zach Thomas and his very pregnant wife, Elizabeth, were chauffeuring Will to his favorite Vietnamese restaurant. As their sensible sedan snaked around the capital via I-35, Will leaned against the backseat window and pointed out landmarks along the way. "And there's the storage space where I keep all my stuff." He sighed. "In between tours I stop in just to say, you know, 'Hello, personal effects.'"

Dessert wasn't going to make Will feel better that day. He'd been on the road for weeks, and his exhausted voice was shifting in and out of Darth Vader mode. His lunch was interrupted by coughing fits and sprints to the bathroom, where we could hear him hacking miserably. At the end of the meal, he paid his share of the bill with wadded dollars and nickels and dimes, and then declared that he would take a vow of silence until his next performance.

We drove in silence to an afternoon show, where the sister-members of CocoRosie alternately sang operatic scales and pounded a toy piano, while Will disinterestedly fashioned himself a badge. From his otherwise empty wallet, he pulled out a pile of cards, which he must have lifted from a florist's counter. They were decorated with daisies and the words, "Thinking of you." Will borrowed a pen to add, ". . . but I can't talk right now. Wish I could!" and crookedly taped the card to his threadbare T-shirt. It stayed there for the rest of the day as he sipped tea from a large silver thermos and wandered through SXSW like a very conspicuous ghost.

Will's vocal recovery was complete by the time Okkervil took the stage on the last night of the festival. His voice was ripe and clear and his songs had never sounded better. Zach smiled widely as he plucked his mandolin strings, and multi-instrumentalist Jonathan Meiberg nearly knocked himself out during a particularly raucous accordion solo. Their hometown crowd went wild, raising their Lone Stars to toast the stage and singing along with every word.

Okkervil River's tour schedule didn't let up, and they began to gather loyal followings in cities far from Austin, but once Zach's baby was born, he couldn't spend as much time on the road as he once did. While the band was weaving through Europe for the first time, home-bound Zach wrote me a note that said, "I dream about the band every night. Is that weird? Last night I dreamt I was trying to turn the van around in a small parking lot and accidentally wrecked it. They had to continue the tour in the only vehicle they could get on short notice: a station wagon."

We can leave the interpretations to the dream analysts, but one thing is clear—despite the poverty, the endless late nights, the fast-food diet, the vows of silence, the couch-surfing, and the whole storage-space-as-home-base issue, being in a band is something lots of people dream about, even the proud young parents among us. That said, even the best tours could be improved by a taste of home now and then.

"This is known in some places as chess pie, but down in Texas we call it buttermilk pie. It is old-fashioned Southern comfort food, and absurdly sweet. I'll give you the recipe as my grandmother gave it to me over the phone when I was just starting out in my dingy little apartment." —ZACH THOMAS

2 eggs

2 tablespoons flour

1 stick of butter or margarine (My grandmother called margarine "oleo." Nowadays, I wouldn't use it on account of all
   the trans fat.)

1¹/₂ cups sugar

³/₄ cup buttermilk

2 teaspoons vanilla extract

1 pie shell

DIRECTIONS:

1. Preheat oven to 350°F.

2. Beat this all up together and pour into the pie shell (from scratch is best, of course).

3. Bake for an hour or until lightly brown on top.

4. Take it out of the oven carefully—the filling may still seem wet, but it should set completely as the pie cools.

Makes 1 pie

from Bryan and Larry's mom, Peggy Herweg

OATMEAL CAKE

Pelican is an atmospheric instrumental quartet, fusing the wonders of earth, space, and post-rock. These guys don't need lyrics to get their point across—on their theatrically titled *The Fire in Our Throats Will Beckon the Thaw*, you'll find slow-burning odes to nature, like "Aurora Borealis," and triumphant seasonal anthems, like "Last Day of Winter." After exposure to the elements on tour, they look forward to comfort food prepared by drummer Larry Herweg and bassist Bryan Herweg's mom. Guitarist Laurent Lebec says, "When Bryan and Larry get off the road, their mom knows to cook up the specials!"

CAKE:

INGREDIENTS:

1 1/4 cups boiling water

1 1/4 cups quick-cooking oats

1/4 pound (one stick) margarine or butter

1 cup brown sugar

1 cup white sugar

1 teaspoon vanilla

2 eggs

1 1/2 cups flour

1/4 teaspoon salt

1 teaspoon cinnamon

1 teaspoon nutmeg

DIRECTIONS:

1. Preheat oven to 350°F.
2. Pour boiling water over oats and let stand for 10 minutes.
3. Blend margarine (or butter) and sugars.
4. Add vanilla, eggs, and dry ingredients.
5. Mix and bake for 35 minutes.

INGREDIENTS:

6 tablespoons of butter, melted

$1/2$ cup brown sugar

$1/4$ cup evaporated milk

$1\,1/2$ cups coconut

DIRECTIONS:

1. Mix and pour over cake.
2. Set in broiler for a minute or two—or just until top bubbles.

Makes 1 cake.

from Margaret White

CHOCOLATE CHIP PIE

When it comes to indie rock, Margaret White gets around. As a multi-instrumentalist (she plays violin, bass, keyboards, banjo, guitar, cello, viola, and jaw harp, and sings, too), Margaret has toured with Cat Power and Belle & Sebastian, and she presently splits her talents between Portastatic and Mascott, and the backing bands of Kevin Devine and Jennifer O'Connor.

Her pie is like a big, fat, delicious chocolate chip cookie, and if you have an electric mixer, it's so easy to make. Throw a party, down a bunch of bourbon, and use the last few drops for this pie. Pop one out of the oven in the wee hours of the morning, and you're the hostess with the mostest. Hands down.

> "Every now and then one of my bands will cook and bake things for practices or recording sessions or sometimes even for shows, I made this once and now am told that I have to make it every time we are planning on baking anything."
>
> —MARGARET WHITE

INGREDIENTS:

1/2 cup butter or margarine, softened

2 eggs, beaten

2 teaspoons vanilla extract or 2 tablespoons bourbon (bourbon is better)

1 cup sugar

1/2 cup flour

1 cup semi-sweet chocolate chips or mini
chips

1 cup chopped walnuts

9-inch graham cracker crust

Whipped cream or ice cream (optional)

DIRECTIONS:

1. Preheat oven to 325°F.
2. With an electric mixer, cream butter until it is light and fluffy.

3. Add eggs and vanilla or bourbon.

4. Combine sugar and flour, and add to the creamed mixture.

5. Stir in chocolate chips and nuts.

6. Pour the mixture into the graham cracker crust.

7. Bake 45 to 50 minutes, or until golden. (You can test it by sticking a toothpick or fork gently into the middle of the pie—it should not come out covered with wet batter but may not necessarily be clean because of the melted chocolate chips.)

8. Cool about one hour (if you can wait that long), and serve warm. Garnish with whipped cream or ice cream if desired.

Makes 1 pie.

from Christopher Paul Richards

VEGAN CHOCOLATE CHIP COOKIES

Wait! I know what you're thinking, but don't turn the page just yet. I, too, believed that there could be no substitute for chocolate chip cookies made with butter and eggs. Then I tried this recipe and watched my boyfriend, a full-fledged carnivore and lover of dairy products, inhale about a dozen vegan cookies in one sitting. I'm not going to tear up my tried-and-true traditional cookie recipe just yet, but I can attest to the goodness of this one from Chris Richards, the former Q and Not U singer who is currently playing solo as Ris Paul Ric. If you're baking for a strict vegan, be sure to avoid milk chocolate and read the fine print to make sure there aren't traces of dairy in your dark or semi-sweet chocolate. If your favorite brand won't cut it, check your local health food store for 100 percent dairy-free chocolate bars and chips from Tropical Source.

"Veganism. For some it's about animal rights. Others eat a vegan diet for their own health. But let's face it, most vegans do it—at least at first—for love. I was already a vegetarian when I met my paramour, a vegan of three years. Our relationship got off to a heated start—even in the kitchen. This woman could cook anything and I played the eager-to-please student.

"Before I knew it I was head over heels—and eating a completely vegan diet. It all happened so fast! I felt excited about my new dietary identity, but also a little helpless. Like my love life had exiled me to a land without milkshakes—a cheerless wasteland where the soy cheese never melts and the cookies are dry and brittle.

"My girlfriend has since taught me how to make delicious fake-shakes and killer vegan pizza—but I have my friend Kirk to thank for the cookies. He brought a bag of these moist marvels to a Ris Paul Ric show in Boston last fall, and I'll be forever grateful. The recipe ain't rocket science, but when you're diving into a brave new dietary world, nothing's more comforting than chocolate-chip cookies."

—CHRIS RICHARDS

1/2 cup organic light brown sugar

1/2 cup organic white sugar

1 cup margarine

1/4 cup soy milk

1 teaspoon vanilla extract

2 1/4 cups unbleached flour

1/2 teaspoon salt

1 teaspoon baking soda

12 ounces dairy-free chocolate chips or chunks

1. Preheat the oven to 350°F.
2. Mix the sugars and the margarine and slowly stir in the soy milk.
3. Fold in the remaining ingredients, except for the chocolate.
4. Add the chocolate chips or chunks.
5. Form the dough into golf ball–sized spheres.
6. Bake those beauties for 8–10 minutes. They're done when they just begin to turn golden—if you wait for them to brown, they'll be extra-crispy.

Substitutions: I highly recommend tinkering with the soy milk and the chocolate. Silk brand soy milk comes in an array of tasty flavors (coffee, chocolate, vanilla, etc.) and all of them work for this recipe. Also, chocolate chips are fine, but I prefer to bust up a fancy-pants dark chocolate bar into pieces. Mint-dark-chocolate? That's what I'm talkin' 'bout!

Makes 3–4 dozen cookies.

from Naoko Yamano

HEALTHY GREEN COOKIES

Shonen Knife, a three-woman Japanese rock trio, started building their song catalogue in the early '90s with quite a few food-centric tunes—they've got odes to strawberry cream puffs, sushi bars, *gyoza* (Chinese dumplings), and even banana chips. Kurt Cobain was among their fans, and he invited them to open a few shows on Nirvana's 1993 *Nevermind* tour. Vocalist and guitarist Naoko Yamano continues to bring her love for food to the stage, and her passion for music to the kitchen. "I like sweets a lot," she admits. "When I have spare time, I occasionally bake cookies. I make various shapes of cookies, like guitar shape, someone's face, etc. It's very fun."

Powdered green tea, or *matcha*, can be very bitter, and Western palates aren't always down with the subtle sweetness of Japanese desserts. To satisfy my own sweet tooth, I like to roll each cookie in sanding sugar before I bake them. Also, it's a little bit of extra work, but if you throw the walnuts in the food processor with the flour, you'll end up with cookies that are chewier and moister, with a marzipan-like flavor. And if you're going that route, you might as well double the recipe—these green tea shortbreads will disappear quickly.

INGREDIENTS:

7 tablespoons of unsalted butter

$4^1/_2$ tablespoons of sugar, sifted

1 cup of cake flour, sifted

$^1/_2$ cup of crushed walnuts

1 teaspoon of baking powder

1 egg

$^1/_2$ teaspoon of vanilla

3 teaspoons of powdered green tea

$^1/_2$ cup sanding sugar (optional)

DIRECTIONS:

1. Preheat oven to 350°F.
2. Mix unsalted butter and sugar.

3. Put all of others and mix.
4. Knead it by hands.
5. Wrap it in cellophane and put it in a refrigerator.
6. Wait one hour (may be playing video games).
7. Roll out dough and mold or cut it into your favorite shapes (and sprinkle the cookies with sanding sugar or roll them in the sugar, if you like).
8. Bake them 10 minutes.

Makes about 2 dozen tablespoon-sized cookies.

from Jamie Williams

"BACON AND EGGS"

In lieu of a drummer, tap dancer Jamie Williams (a former model, pro ballerina, and grade-school teacher) keeps the beat for Tilly and the Wall. Jamie was once in a little Omaha band called Park Ave., featuring Conor Oberst (pre-Bright Eyes) and Clark Baechle (pre-Faint), and her current band's debut, *Wild Like Children*, was the first release on Oberst's own label, Team Love. The band's giddy sound finds its way into this wacky party snack/dessert recipe. Jamie says, "While driving in our luxurious, forest green conversion van, we often find ourselves having long, intense conversations about just how delish these bacon and eggs really are."

> "[Must be read in a funny, inside your head, mad scientist-type voice.]
>
> "La la la!!! Now bacon and eggs may sound sort of gross for dessert, but we think you'll be pleasantly surprised—and dubbed 'the life of the frickin' party'—when you bring this tasty treat to your next gathering. Even your children will love them! It's like a toy you can eat."
> —JAMIE WILLIAMS

YOU WILL NEED . . .

INGREDIENTS:

a shitload of those small straight pretzels
————————— (◄—about that big)
some white chocolate (usually found in a
brick in the baking section)

a crap-ton of yelow M&M'S (some green
ones too if you're feeling frisky)
some wax paper to cover your work surface

DIRECTIONS:

1. Start by laying out wax paper over a cookie sheet. Take one, two, or three pretzels (bacon), and lay them side by side somewhere in a group on the wax paper. We like two

the best, but you can do however many you want. Do this a bunch of times, that's how many you'll have.

2. Then, use a double boiler to melt some white chocolate. You can make your own double boiler by getting a pot of water and putting a heat-safe bowl into the water. You'll put the chocolate in the bowl and the heat from the water will melt the chocolate. The water should be simmering beneath. When the chocolate has melted and is silky when stirred, it's ready!

3. Take a spoonful of chocolate and drip a circle of it on the pretzels, somewhere in the middle of them. This is your egg white! It shouldn't be perfect, so don't worry about that. After you drip chocolate on one, right away you should place one or two yellow M&M'S on the "egg whites."

These are your yolks!!! FUN! It can be really witty for you to use green M&M'S for green eggs. So, do it, be very witty. Also, remember to put the "M&M" side down, otherwise it looks ghetto. Feel free to use any type of M&M'S too, peanut, peanut butter, or the mini ones are all radical. After you add all your yolks, put the whole cookie sheet in the fridge so the white chocolate hardens. Now, go have fun, these are really terribly cute and so so so yummy. XOXOXOXO

from Brendan Bayliss

KAHLÚA CAKE

When I was in college at Notre Dame, the majority of undergrad musicians were playing lo-fi covers of Dave Matthews and Barenaked Ladies songs. Naïve as I was, I assumed that people from small Midwestern towns simply hadn't been exposed to indie rock. I altruistically lent out my Lemonheads and Archers of Loaf CDs, but they were promptly handed back with perplexed expressions. I wept, bought a pair of big headphones, and got a job projecting movies on Friday and Saturday nights to make the lonely weekends go by faster. Eventually, I met an older, cooler film major named Sean, who introduced me to a band that was always hanging out on his front porch, Umphrey's McGee. Say what you will about their presence in an indie rock cookbook, but this jam band made my life worth living. My fondest memories of South Bend, Indiana, take me back to the State Theater where Umphrey's—who were also pretty big on covers at the time—would spice up Beatles medleys with frantic light shows and endless guitar noodling. These guys still make me want to wrap a bandana around my head and dance around in flip-flops.

The recipe for this irresistibly moist Bundt cake was passed along from lead vocalist and guitarist Brendan Bayliss. The pound of sour cream in the ingredients list may seem extreme, but don't skimp. In the words of their always-in-tow soundman, Kevin Browning, "This cake is obscenely good."

INGREDIENTS:

1 package chocolate fudge "pudding in the mix" cake mix

16 ounces sour cream

1/4 cup of vegetable oil

2 eggs

1/2 cup of Kahlúa

12 ounces chocolate chips

1. Preheat oven to 325°F.
2. Grease your Bundt pan.
3. Blend all ingredients with mixer and pour into pan.
4. Bake 45–55 minutes.
5. Let the cake cool in the pan for at least 15 minutes before you flip it.
6. Sit down and eat half the cake.

Makes 1 cake.

INDEX

A

Abell, Geoff, 110

Africanitas Ricas, 203–4

Aioli-Garlic Mayo, 52

Alaska-Style Macaroni Soup *al Carne,* 84–88

Alexandra, 99

Aloha, 97

Aluminum Group, 75

Amphetameanies, 61, 62

Anderson, Reid, 136

appetizers, 20

    Asparagus Side Dish/Antipasto, 113–14

    Baked Brie, 32–33

    Best Guacamole Ever, 55–56

    Bill's *Pico de Gallo,* 34

    Hott Boiled Peanuts, 56–57

    Life of the Party Chicken on a Stick, 53–54

    Roasted Bone Marrow "Battles Style," 21–23

    Rock 'n' Roll Rangoon, 40–41

    The Scoville Tortilla, 50–52

    The Secret Tobias Family Potato Pancake Recipe, 46–47

Apple Quiche Puffs, Big, 4–5

Archers of Loaf, 119, 234

Arroz con Pollo, Spicy, 99–100

Asian Stir-Fry for Vegetarians Who Hate Vegetables, 169–70

asparagus:

    Side Dish/Antipasto, 113–14

    Swanky Mac and Cheese, 126–28

avocados:

    Best Guacamole Ever, 55–56

    Fish Tacos with Avocados,
        129–30

    Foreign Chicken Dinner, 112–14

    Pear and Goat Cheese *Panini,* 68

    Sweet Potato Biscuits and Vegan
    Vegetable Gravy, 11–14

    Sweet Potato-Mango-Chicken
        Quesadillas, 110–11

    Thor's Black Bean Nachos, 171–72

    Uncle Kyle's Avocado Tacos, 151

B

Baby, 32

Bachmann, Eric, 119

bacon:

    Big Apple Quiche Puffs, 4–5

    Exploding Sandwich, 65–66

"Bacon and Eggs," 232–33

Bad Plus, 136

Baechle, Clark, 232

Baked Barbecue Tofu, 142–43

Baked Brie, 32–33

Balllance, Laura, 173

bananas:

    Africanitas Ricas, 203–4

    Sissy's Banana Pudding, 205–8

Banhart, Devendra, 151, 203

Banks, Paul, 214

Barbecue Tofu, Baked, 142–43

Battles, 21

Bauer, Peter, 112

Bayliss, Brendan, 234

BBQ Steak, 79–80

beans:

    Cheesy Sleazy, 15–16

    Ham-Feta-Beanie, 61

    Peanutty Black-Bean Tofu, 178–79

    Thor's Black Bean Nachos, 171–72

beans, garbanzo (chickpeas):

    Eddie Vedder Stew, 147

    Kudzu Kurry, 149

    Quick Chickpeas, 165–66

Beatty, Marc, 30

Bedsworth, Brian, 34

beef:

    Alaska-Style Macaroni Soup *al Carne,*
        84–88

    BBQ Steak, 79–80

    Roasted Bone Marrow "Battles Style,"
        21–23

    Sauerbraten, 91–92

Bell, Hudson, 67

Belle & Sebastian, 61, 62, 226

Bergsman, Victoria, 140

Best Guacamole Ever, 55–56

Big Apple Quiche Puffs, 4–5

Bill's *Pico de Gallo,* 34

Birds of Avalon, 24

biscuits:

    Big Apple Quiche Puffs, 4–5

    Fried Chicken with Biscuits and Gravy,
        97–98

biscuits *(continued)*:

Sweet Potato Biscuits and Vegan
Vegetable Gravy, 11–14

Black Hollies, 27

Bling Kong, 4

Boar, Wild, Ragú, 95–96

Boe, Eirik Glambek, 122

Bologna, Mustard, and Pickle Sandwich, 63

Bone Marrow, Roasted, "Battles Style,"
21–23

Brakes, 30

Brandy Peach Sauce for Chicken or Tofu,
103–4

Bratmobile, 183

Bratwurst, Midwestern-Style, 81–83

Braxton, Tyondai, 21

Bread, Mom's Muffin, 7–8

breakfast, 2–3

Big Apple Quiche Puffs, 4–5

Cheesy Sleazy, 15–16

Mom's Muffin Bread, 7–8

Southern Cheese Grits, 9–10

Sweet Potato Biscuits and Vegan
Vegetable Gravy, 11–14

Tofu Scramble, 6

Varldens Basta Pannkaka, 17–18

Brie, Baked, 32–33

Bright Eyes, 69, 232

British Sea Power, 30

broccoli:

Healthy Green Soup, 30–31

Kudzu Kurry, 149

Sweet Potato Biscuits and Vegan
Vegetable Gravy, 11–14

Broccoli Rabe, *Orecchiette* with, 136–37

Browning, Kevin, 234

Brussels Sprouts à la Denzel Washington,
35–37

Bryant, Jenn, 205–6

Burns, Joey, 6

Burtch, Aaron, 79

Buscemi, Steve, 65

Butler, Julie, 218

Butler, Syd, 218

Buttermilk Pie, 221–23

butterscotch:

Butterscotch Pie, 218

7-Layer Bars, 219–20

C

Cacao Rosso, 214–15

cake:

Chocolate Worm, 211–12

Kahlúa Cake, 234–35

Oatmeal Cake, 224–25

Strawberry Pop Cake, 201–2

Calexico, 6

Camera Obscura, 138

Camiloflage, 185–86

Camu Tao, 131

Capsize 7, 110

Caraeff, Ezra, 132

carrots:

Eddie Vedder Stew, 147

carrots (*continued*):
Kudzu Kurry, 149
Caswell, Dennis, 42
Catfish Haven, 201
cauliflower:
Eddie Vedder Stew, 147
Kudzu Kurry, 149
Tato Mato, 160–62
Centro-matic, 117
Champale, 154
cheese:
Alaska-Style Macaroni Soup *al Carne*, 84–88
Baked Brie, 32–33
Big Apple Quiche Puffs, 4–5
Cheesy Sleazy, 15–16
Eggplant Parmesan, 144–46
El Hefe's Specialties, 89–90
Ham-Feta-Beanie, 61
HRT – Halloumi, Radicchio, and Tomato Sandwich, 62
Night-Before-Tour Mac and Cheese, 154–56
Pear and Goat Cheese *Panini,* 68
Riverboats, 67
Rock 'n' Roll Rangoon, 40–41
Southern Cheese Grits, 9–10
Spinach Lasagna, 152–53
Swanky Mac and Cheese, 126–28
Sweet Potato-Mango-Chicken Quesadillas, 110–11
Thor's Black Bean Nachos, 171–72

Tomato Sauce for Pasta, 140–41
Vegetable Enchiladas with Homemade Tomatillo Salsa, 157–59
The "You Can Care If You Wanna" Sandwich, 71–72
Zucchini Slippers, 48–49
Cheesy Sleazy, 15–16
Cherry, Matt, 9
Cherry Valence, 24
chicken:
Brandy Peach Sauce for Chicken, 103–4
Chicken Filo Pesto Parcel with Puy Puy, 105–7
Chicken in Coconut Curry, 101–2
Exploding Sandwich, 65–66
Foreign Chicken Dinner, 112–14
Fried Chicken with Biscuits and Gravy, 97–98
Kudzu Kurry, 149
Life of the Party Chicken on a Stick, 53–54
Potpie, 167–68
Rock 'n' Ramen, 108–9
Spicy Arroz con Pollo, 99–100
Spicy Wings à la Chickie, 115–16
Sweet Potato-Mango-Chicken Quesadillas, 110–11
chickpeas (garbanzo beans):
Eddie Vedder Stew, 147
Kudzu Kurry, 149
Quick Chickpeas, 165–66

chili:

    Alaska-Style Macaroni Soup *al Carne,* 84–88

    El Hefe's Specialties, 89–90

chocolate:

    Cacao Rosso, 214–15

    Chocolate Balls, 199–200

    Chocolate Chip Pie, 226–27

    Chocolate Worm, 211–12

    Kahlúa Cake, 234–35

    7-Layer Bars, 219–20

    Vegan Chocolate Chip Cookies, 228–29

Cinemechanica, 46

Clam Chowder Sauce, Spaghetti with, 132

Cline, Patsy, 188

Cobain, Kurt, 230

Cobbler, One-Dish Fresh-Fruit, 216–17

coconut:

    Chicken in Coconut Curry, 101–2

    Seared Tuna with Wasabi-Coconut Sauce and Roasted-Pepper Rice Pilaf, 119–21

    7-Layer Bars, 219–20

    Tim Curry, 149–50

Cohen, Andy, 15

Collard Greens, Not-So-Greasy, 24–26

Concretes, 140

Contraband, 46

Convertino, John, 6

Cooke, Mick, 61, 62

cookies:

    Cacao Rosso, 214–15

Healthy Green Cookies, 230–31

    Vegan Chocolate Chip Cookies, 228–29

corn:

    El Hefe's Specialties, 89–90

    Tofu Potpie, 167–68

Countrypolitan, 193

Crisp, Kelly, 48

Crooked Fingers, 119

curry:

    Chicken in Coconut Curry, 101–2

    Curry Variations, 148–50

D

Dahlquist, Michael, 15

Dale, Mark, 46

Dälek, 99

Dando, Evan, 34, 199

D'Angelo, Pete, 144

Dark 'n' Stormy Florida, 188–89

Darnielle, John, 160

Death Cab for Cutie, 17, 64

Decemberists, 77

Deitz, Casey, 132

Descendents, 34

desserts, 198

    Africanitas Ricas, 203–4

    "Bacon and Eggs," 232–33

    Buttermilk Pie, 221–23

    Butterscotch Pie, 218

    Cacao Rosso, 214–15

    Chocolate Balls, 199–200

    Chocolate Chip Pie, 226–27

desserts *(continued)*:
    Chocolate Worm, 211–12
    Healthy Green Cookies, 230–31
    Kahlúa Cake, 234–35
    Lemon Ginger Flapjacks, 209–10
    Oatmeal Cake, 224–25
    One-Dish Fresh-Fruit Cobbler, 216–17
    Pecan Pie, 213
    7-Layer Bars, 219–20
    Sissy's Banana Pudding, 205–8
    Strawberry Pop Cake, 201–2
    Vegan Chocolate Chip Cookies,
       228–29
Devine, Kevin, 226
Dirty Snowflake, 187
Disband, 46
Don Caballero, 21
Doughman, David, 192
Dr. Dog, 7
drinks, 182
    Camiloflage, 185–86
    The Countrypolitan, 193
    Dark 'n' Stormy Florida, 188–89
    Dirty Snowflake, 187
    Florida East Coast Champion Sweet Tea,
       189–90
    The John Glenn, 192
    The Karate Kid, 184
    Margaritas, 78
    Party At Your Own Risk Sangria, 183
    Patriot Act *Mojitos,* 191
    Vegan Sky Juice, 194–95

Drive-By Truckers, 205
Droste, Ed, 213
Dunbar, Gavin, 138

E

Early Day Miners, 184
Eddie Vedder Stew, 147
eggplant:
    Eggplant Parmesan, 144–46
    Kudzu Kurry, 149
eggs:
    Big Apple Quiche Puffs, 4–5
    Cheesy Sleazy, 15–16
    The Scoville Tortilla, 50–52
El Hefe, 89
El Hefe's Specialties, 89–90
Elmore, Elizabeth, 169
El-P, 131
Enchiladas, Vegetable, with Homemade
    Tomatillo Salsa, 157–59
Enon, 38
Exploding Sandwich, 65–66

F

Faint, 232
Fein, Erin, 40
Feta-Ham-Beanie, 61
Field, Kyle, 151
Finn, Craig, 81
fish and seafood:
    Fish Tacos with Avocados, 129–30
    Rooftop Party Salmon, 131

fish and seafood *(continued)*:

Seared Tuna with Wasabi-Coconut Sauce and Roasted-Pepper Rice Pilaf, 119–21

South San Gabriel Sweet Potatoes and Salmon, 117–18

Spaghetti with Clam Chowder Sauce, 132

Swanky Mac and Cheese, 126–28

Tropical Fish Tacos, 124–25

Wolf Fish *a l'Italia,* 122–23

Flansburgh, John, 193

Florida East Coast Champion Sweet Tea, 189–90

Fogarino, Sam, 214

Foreign Chicken Dinner, 112–14

Forms, 185

Franz Ferdinand, 61, 209

Frazier, Kathryn, 131

Fried Chicken with Biscuits and Gravy, 97–98

Frog Eyes, 211

Fruit, Fresh, One-Dish Cobbler, 216–17

G

garbanzo beans (chickpeas):

Eddie Vedder Stew, 147

Kudzu Kurry, 149

Quick Chickpeas, 165–66

Gardner, Kori, 68

garlic:

Aioli-Garlic Mayo, 52

Garlic Mushy Peas, 42–43

A Recipe for the One Who Is Getting Some Kind of Cold, 38–39

Gibbard, Ben, 64

ginger:

Lemon Ginger Flapjacks, 209–10

A Recipe for the One Who Is Getting Some Kind of Cold, 38–39

Goat Cheese and Pear *Panini,* 68

Gonnelli, Jon, 93

Goodmark, Robyn, 219

Goswell, Rachel, 44, 105, 106

Grandaddy, 79

gravy:

Fried Chicken with Biscuits and Gravy, 97–98

Sweet Potato Biscuits and Vegan Vegetable Gravy, 11–14

Greens, Not-So-Greasy, 24–26

Grits, Southern Cheese, 9–10

Grizzly Bear, 213

Guacamole, Best Ever, 55–56

H

Halloumi, Radicchio, and Tomato Sandwich, 62

Halstead, Neil, 44

ham:

Ham-Feta-Beanie, 61

Riverboats, 67

Hamilton, Eamon, 30

Hammel, Jason, 68

Harmer, Nick, 64

Harrington, Tim, 218

Harris, Thor, 171

Hatstat, Joel, 46

"Have Mercy on Me" Lentil Soup,
    27–29

Hayden, 65

Headlights, 40

Healthy Green Cookies, 230–31

Healthy Green Soup, 30–31

Hefe, El, 89

Helmet, 21

Hepler, James, 53

Herweg, Bryan, 224

Herweg, Larry, 224

Herweg, Peggy, 224

Heston Rifle, 142

Hold Steady, 81

Holy Childhood, 194

Hood, Patterson, 205

Hott Boiled Peanuts, 56–57

Houston McCoy, 144

Howard, Ivan, 48

HRT—Halloumi, Radicchio, and Tomato
    Sandwich, 62

Hunter, George, 201

Hunter, María, 201

I

Imperial Teen, 147

Interpol, 214

Irving, 187

Isleib, Drew, 101

J

James, Jim, 71

John Glenn, 192

Johnson, Will, 117

K

Kahlúa:
    Dirty Snowflake, 187
    Kahlúa Cake, 234–35

Kapranos, Alex, 61, 209

Karate Kid, 184

Kenny, Brendan, 185

Kenny, Jackson, 185

Keri's Vegan Greek Sandwiches,
    69–70

Kiley, Jake, 108

Kings of Convenience, 122

Komakino, 42

Konopka, David, 21

Kubler, Tad, 81

Kudzu Wish, 148

Kumar, Cheetie, 24

Kweller, Ben, 199

Kweller, Liz, 199

L

LaFollette, Timothy, 148

Lasagna, Spinach, 152–53

Lebec, Laurent, 224

Leek & Potato Soup, 44–45

Leithauser, Hamilton, 112

LeMaster, Andy, 165

Lemon Ginger Flapjacks, 209–10

Lemonheads, 34, 199, 234

lentils:

    "Have Mercy on Me" Lentil Soup, 27–29

    Puy Puy, 106–7

Leo, Chris, 194–95

Leo, Danny, 194

Leo, Ted, 175, 194

Lerner, Dave, 175–76

Les Savy Fav, 218

Lewis, Jenny, 69

Life of the Party Chicken on a Stick, 53–54

Linnell, John, 193

Little Wings, 151

Long Winters, 84

Lorca, Daniel, 191

Lucero, 152

Lynne, Jeff, 69

Lynx, 21

M

macaroni:

    Alaska-Style Macaroni Soup *al Carne,*
      84–88

    El Hefe's Specialties, 89–90

    Night-Before-Tour Mac and Cheese,
      154–56

    Swanky Mac and Cheese, 126–28

McGerr, Jason, 17, 64

main courses for carnivores, 74

    Alaska-Style Macaroni Soup *al Carne,*
      84–88

BBQ Steak, 79–80

Bologna, Mustard, and Pickle Sandwich,
    63

Brandy Peach Sauce for Chicken, 103–4

Chicken Filo Pesto Parcel with Puy Puy,
    105–7

Chicken in Coconut Curry, 101–2

El Hefe's Specialties, 89–90

Exploding Sandwich, 65–66

Fish Tacos with Avocados, 129–30

Foreign Chicken Dinner, 112–14

Fried Chicken with Biscuits and Gravy,
    97–98

Ham-Feta-Beanie, 61

Midwestern-Style Bratwurst, 81–83

Pasta Bolognese, 75–76

Pork Chops Salvemini, 93–94

Pork Loin with Poblano Chilies, 77–78

Riverboats, 67

Rock 'n' Ramen, 108–9

Rooftop Party Salmon, 131

Sauerbraten, 91–92

Seared Tuna with Wasabi-Coconut Sauce
    and Roasted-Pepper Rice Pilaf, 119–21

South San Gabriel Sweet Potatoes and
    Salmon, 117–18

Spaghetti with Clam Chowder Sauce, 132

Spicy Arroz con Pollo, 99–100

Spicy Wings à la Chickie, 115–16

Swanky Mac and Cheese, 126–28

Sweet Potato-Mango-Chicken Quesadillas,
    110–11

main courses for vegetarians *(continued)*:

Tropical Fish Tacos, 124–25

Wild Boar Ragú, 95–96

Wolf Fish *a l'Italia,* 122–23

Asian Stir-Fry for Vegetarians Who Hate
Vegetables, 169–70

Baked Barbecue Tofu, 142–43

Brandy Peach Sauce for Tofu, 103–4

Curry Variations, 148–50

Eddie Vedder Stew, 147

Eggplant Parmesan, 144–46

El Hefe's Specialties, 89–90

Ham-Feta-Beanie, 61

HRT – Halloumi, Radicchio, and Tomato
Sandwich, 62

Keri's Vegan Greek Sandwiches, 69–70

Night-Before-Tour Mac and Cheese,
154–56

Orecchiette with Broccoli Rabe, 136–37

Peanutty Black-Bean Tofu, 178–79

Pear and Goat Cheese *Panini,* 68

Quick Chickpeas, 165–66

The Scoville Tortilla, 50–52

The Secret Tobias Family Potato Pancake
Recipe, 46–47

Semi-Raw Everyday Pasta, 175–77

Spiced Tofu Stir-Fry, 163–64

Spinach Lasagna, 152–53

Sweet Potato-Mango Quesadillas, 110–11

Tato Mato, 160–62

"Thai" Grilled Marinated Tofu, 173–74

Thor's Black Bean Nachos, 171–72

Tofu Potpie, 167–68

Tofu Scramble, 6

Tomato Sauce for Pasta, 140–41

Uncle Kyle's Avocado Tacos, 151

Vegetable Enchiladas with Homemade
Tomatillo Salsa, 157–59

Vegetarian Paella, 138–39

Veggie Sausage and Peanut Butter
Sandwich, 64

The "You Can Care If You Wanna"
Sandwich, 71–72

Zucchini Slippers, 48–49

Mango-Sweet Potato-Chicken Quesadillas,
110–11

Maplewood, 154

Margaritas, 78

Mascott, 226

Maserati, 9, 40

Mates of State, 68

Matz, Dan, 115

Mayo, Aioli-Garlic, 52

meat:

Alaska-Style Macaroni Soup *al Carne,*
84–88

BBQ Steak, 79–80

Bologna, Mustard, and Pickle Sandwich,
63

El Hefe's Specialties, 89–90

Exploding Sandwich, 65–66

Life of the Party Pork on a Stick, 53–54

Midwestern-Style Bratwurst, 81–83

Pasta Bolognese, 75–76

meat *(continued)*:

    Pork Chops Salvemini, 93–94

    Pork Loin with Poblano Chilies,
        77–78

    Potpie, 167–68

    Riverboats, 67

    Roasted Bone Marrow "Battles Style,"
        21–23

    Sauerbraten, 91–92

    Wild Boar Ragú, 95–96

Meiberg, Jonathan, 222

Mercer, Carey, 211

Meringue, 207–8

Midwestern-Style Bratwurst, 81–83

Miller, Kathy, 7

Miller, Zach, 7

Mills, Chris, 63

Minor, Laura, 188

Mobius Band, 124

Mojave 3, 44, 105

Mojitos, Patriot Act, 191

Momin, Alap, 99

Mom's Muffin Bread, 7–8

Morey, Justin Angelo, 27

Mountain Goats, 160

Murder by Death, 163

Musick, Jackie, 11, 12

mushrooms:

    Foreign Chicken Dinner, 112–14

    Sweet Potato Biscuits and Vegan
        Vegetable Gravy, 11–14

My Morning Jacket, 69, 71

N

Nachos, Thor's Black Bean, 171–72

Nada Surf, 191

Nagler, Judah, 132

Navin, Frank, 75

Navin, John, 75

Neuman, Molly, 183

Nichols, Ben, 152

Night-Before-Tour Mac and Cheese,
    154–56

NOFX, 89

noodles, *see* pasta and noodles

Northern State, 219

Not-So-Greasy Greens, 24–26

Now It's Overhead, 165

nuts:

    Chocolate Balls, 199–200

    Chocolate Chip Pie, 226–27

    Healthy Green Cookies, 230–31

    Pecan Pie, 213

    Semi-Raw Everyday Pasta, 175–77

    7-Layer Bars, 219–20

O

oats:

    Lemon Ginger Flapjacks, 209–10

    Oatmeal Cake, 224–25

Oberst, Conor, 232

Oberst, Matt, 53

O'Connor, Jennifer, 226

Okkervil River, 221

Oktopus, 99

One-Dish Fresh-Fruit Cobbler, 216–17
Orecchiette with Broccoli Rabe, 136–37

P

Paella, Vegetarian, 138–39
pancakes:
    The Secret Tobias Family Potato Pancake
        Recipe, 46–47
    Varldens Basta Pannkaka, 17–18
Panini, Pear and Goat Cheese, 68
Park Ave., 232
Parks, Cale, 97
Party At Your Own Risk Sangria, 183
pasta and noodles:
    Alaska-Style Macaroni Soup *al Carne,*
        84–88
    El Hefe's Specialties, 89–90
    Night-Before-Tour Mac and Cheese,
        154–56
    Orecchiette with Broccoli Rabe, 136–37
    Pasta Bolognese, 75–76
    Rock 'n' Ramen, 108–9
    Semi-Raw Everyday Pasta, 175–77
    Spaghetti with Clam Chowder Sauce,
        132
    Spinach Lasagna, 152–53
    Swanky Mac and Cheese, 126–28
    Tomato Sauce for Pasta, 140–41
    Wild Boar Ragú, 95–96
    Wolf Fish *a l'Italia,* 122–23
Patriot Act *Mojitos,* 191
peaches:

Brandy Peach Sauce for Chicken or Tofu,
    103–4
One-Dish Fresh-Fruit Cobbler, 216–17
peanut butter:
    Peanut Butter and Veggie Sausage
        Sandwich, 64
    Peanutty Black-Bean Tofu, 178–79
Peanuts, Hott Boiled, 56–57
Pear and Goat Cheese *Panini,* 68
peas:
    Bombay Tim's Hot-Ass Vegan Curry, 150
    Garlic Mushy Peas, 42–43
    Tato Mato, 160–62
    Tofu Potpie, 167–68
    Vegetarian Paella, 138–39
pecans:
    Chocolate Balls, 199–200
    Pecan Pie, 213
    7-Layer Bars, 219–20
Pegasuses-XL, 46
Pelican, 224
peppers, bell:
    Bombay Tim's Hot-Ass Vegan Curry, 150
    Kudzu Kurry, 149
    Seared Tuna with Wasabi-Coconut Sauce
        and Roasted-Pepper Rice Pilaf, 119–21
Phelan, Patrick, 126
Pico de Gallo, Bill's, 34
pie:
    Buttermilk Pie, 221–23
    Butterscotch Pie, 218
    Chocolate Chip Pie, 226–27

pie *(continued)*:

    Pecan Pie, 213

    Tofu Potpie, 167–68

Pilato, Victoria "Rifle," 142, 163

Polivka, Galen, 81–82

Pollard, Robert, 173

Pond, Matt, 157–58

pork:

    Life of the Party Pork on a Stick, 53–54

    Pork Chops Salvemini, 93–94

    Pork Loin with Poblano Chilies, 77–78

Potash, Julie, 219

Portastatic, 226

potatoes:

    Bombay Tim's Hot-Ass Vegan Curry, 150

    Eddie Vedder Stew, 147

    Leek & Potato Soup, 44–45

    The Scoville Tortilla, 50–52

    The Secret Tobias Family Potato Pancake
        Recipe, 46–47

    Tato Mato, 160–62

    Tofu Potpie, 167–68

Potpie, Tofu, 167–68

poultry, *see* chicken

Power, Cat, 226

Pudding, Sissy's Banana, 205–8

Puy Puy, 106–7

Q

Query, Nate, 77

Quesadillas, Sweet Potato-Mango-Chicken,
    110–11

Quiche Puffs, Big Apple, 4–5

Quick Chickpeas, 165–66

R

Racebannon, 103, 167

Radicchio, Halloumi, and Tomato Sandwich,
    62

Rahim, 91

Rapider Than Horsepower, 103, 167

A Recipe for the One Who Is Getting Some
    Kind of Cold, 38–39

Reputation, 169

rice:

    Asian Stir-Fry for Vegetarians Who Hate
        Vegetables, 169–70

    Foreign Chicken Dinner, 112–14

    Kudzu Kurry, 149

    Peanutty Black-Bean Tofu,
        178–79

    Seared Tuna with Wasabi-Coconut Sauce
        and Roasted-Pepper Rice Pilaf,
        119–21

    Spicy Arroz con Pollo, 99–100

    Tato Mato, 160–62

    Tim Curry, 149–50

    Vegetarian Paella, 138–39

Richards, Christopher Paul, 228

Richardson, Jonathan, 184

Rilo Kiley, 69

Ris Paul Ric, 228

Ritchie, Brian, 95

Riverboats, 67

RJD2, 129

Roasted Bone Marrow "Battles Style," 21–23

Robinson, Anita and Kevin, 55

Rock 'n' Ramen, 108–9

Rock 'n' Roll Rangoon, 40–41

Roderick, John, 84–87

Rooftop Party Salmon, 131

Roots of Orchis, 11

Rosebuds, 48

Rozzo, Mark, 154

Rye Coalition, 93

s

Saligoe, Chris, 103, 167

salmon:

    Rooftop Party Salmon, 131

    South San Gabriel Sweet Potatoes and
        Salmon, 117–18

salsa:

    Bill's *Pico de Gallo,* 34

    Thor's Black Bean Nachos, 171–72

    Tomatillo Salsa, 158

Salvemini, Nick, 93

sandwiches, 60

    Baked Barbecue Tofu, 142–43

    Bologna, Mustard, and Pickle Sandwich,
        63

    Exploding Sandwich, 65–66

    Ham-Feta-Beanie, 61

    HRT—Halloumi, Radicchio, and Tomato
        Sandwich, 62

    Keri's Vegan Greek Sandwiches, 69–70

Midwestern-Style Bratwurst, 81–83

Pear and Goat Cheese *Panini,* 68

Riverboats, 67

Veggie Sausage and Peanut Butter
    Sandwich, 64

The "You Can Care If You Wanna"
    Sandwich, 71–72

Sangria, Party At Your Own Risk, 183

S.A. Smash, 131

sauces:

    Aioli-Garlic Mayo, 52

    Basic Curry Sauce, 148

    Brandy Peach Sauce for Chicken or Tofu,
        103–4

    Tomato Sauce for Pasta, 140–41

Sauerbraten, 91–92

sausage:

    Midwestern-Style Bratwurst, 81–83

    Vegetarian Paella, 138–39

    Veggie Sausage and Peanut Butter
        Sandwich, 64

Schroeter, Liz "Shredder," 4

Scott, Steven, 187

The Scoville Tortilla, 50–52

Scoville Unit, 50

seafood, *see* fish and seafood

Seared Tuna with Wasabi-Coconut Sauce and
    Roasted-Pepper Rice Pilaf, 119–21

The Secret Tobias Family Potato Pancake
    Recipe, 46–47

Sedgwick, Edie, 35

Semi-Raw Everyday Pasta, 175–77

Senés, Tony, 50

7-Layer Bars, 219–20

Shearwater, 171

Sheff, Will, 221–22

Shonen Knife, 230

Shudder to Think, 32

side dishes, 20

    Asparagus Side Dish/Antipasto, 113–14

    Brussels Sprouts à la Denzel Washington, 35–37

    Garlic Mushy Peas, 42–43

    Not-So-Greasy Greens, 24–26

    Puy Puy, 106–7

    Zucchini Slippers, 48–49

Siler, Paul, 24

Silkworm, 15

Simon, Matt, 178

Sissy's Banana Pudding, 205–8

Slowdive, 44, 105

Smoosh, 17

Sorry About Dresden, 53

soups, 20

    Alaska-Style Macaroni Soup *al Carne*, 84–88

    "Have Mercy on Me" Lentil Soup, 27–29

    Healthy Green Soup, 30–31

    Leek & Potato Soup, 44–45

    A Recipe for the One Who Is Getting Some Kind of Cold, 38–39

Southern Cheese Grits, 9–10

South San Gabriel Sweet Potatoes and Salmon, 117–18

Spaghetti with Clam Chowder Sauce, 132

Spero, Correne "Guinea Love," 219

Spiced Tofu Stir-Fry, 163–64

Spicy Arroz con Pollo, 99–100

Spicy Wings à la Chickie, 115–16

spinach:

    Bombay Tim's Hot-Ass Vegan Curry, 150

    Not-So-Greasy Greens, 24–26

    Peanutty Black-Bean Tofu, 178–79

    Seared Tuna with Wasabi-Coconut Sauce and Roasted-Pepper Rice Pilaf, 119–21

    Spinach Lasagna, 152–53

    Tofu Scramble, 6

    Wolf Fish *a l'Italia,* 122–23

squash:

    Chicken Filo Pesto Parcel with Puy Puy, 105–7

    Kudzu Kurry, 149

    Spiced Tofu Stir-Fry, 163–64

    Tofu Scramble, 6

    Vegetable Enchiladas with Homemade Tomatillo Salsa, 157–59

    Zucchini Slippers, 48–49

Stanier, John, 21

Staples, Josh, 132

starters, *see* appetizers

Steak, BBQ, 79–80

Stebbins, Jone, 147

Sterling, Ben, 124

Stevenson, Bill, 34

Stew, Eddie Vedder, 147

stir-fry:

    Asian Stir-Fry for Vegetarians Who Hate
        Vegetables, 169–70

stir-fry *(continued)*:

    Spiced Tofu Stir-Fry, 163–64

strawberry(ies):

    Cacao Rosso, 214–15

    Strawberry Pop Cake, 201–2

Strung Out, 108

Superchunk, 173

Surgeson, Clare, 117

Sutton, George, 91

Sutton, Phil, 91

Swanky Mac and Cheese, 126–28

Swearing at Motorists, 192

sweet potatoes:

    South San Gabriel Sweet Potatoes and
        Salmon, 117–18

    Sweet Potato Biscuits and Vegan
        Vegetable Gravy, 11–14

sweet potatoes *(continued)*:

    Sweet Potato-Mango-Chicken
        Quesadillas, 110–11

    Tim Curry, 149–50

T

tacos:

    Fish Tacos with Avocados, 129–30

    Tropical Fish Tacos, 124–25

    Uncle Kyle's Avocado Tacos, 151

Tato Mato, 160–62

tea:

    Florida East Coast Champion Sweet Tea,
        189–90

    Healthy Green Cookies, 230–31

Ted Leo and the Pharmacists, 175, 194

Teres, Ecco, 185

"Thai" Grilled Marinated Tofu, 173–74

They Might Be Giants, 193

Thomas, Zach, 221, 222

Thor's Black Bean Nachos, 171–72

tilapia:

    Fish Tacos with Avocados, 129–30

    Tropical Fish Tacos, 124–25

Tilly and the Wall, 232

Tobias, Jeff, 46

Tobias, Mel, 46

tofu:

    Baked Barbecue Tofu, 142–43

    Bombay Tim's Hot-Ass Vegan Curry,
        150

    Brandy Peach Sauce for Tofu, 103–4

    Kudzu Kurry, 149

    Peanutty Black-Bean Tofu, 178–79

    A Recipe for the One Who Is Getting
        Some Kind of Cold, 38–39

    Spiced Tofu Stir-Fry, 163–64

    "Thai" Grilled Marinated Tofu, 173–74

    Tim Curry, 149–50

    Tofu Potpie, 167–68

    Tofu Scramble, 6

    Vegetarian Paella, 138–39

Tomahawk, 21

Tomatillo Salsa, Homemade, Vegetable
  Enchiladas with, 157–59

tomato(es):

  Best Guacamole Ever, 55–56

tomato(es) *(continued)*:

  Bill's *Pico de Gallo,* 34

  Bombay Tim's Hot-Ass Vegan Curry, 150

  Chicken in Coconut Curry, 101–2

  Eddie Vedder Stew, 147

  Eggplant Parmesan, 144–46

  HRT—Halloumi, Radicchio, and
    Tomato Sandwich, 62

  Pasta Bolognese, 75–76

  Spinach Lasagna, 152–53

  Tato Mato, 160–62

  Tomato Sauce for Pasta, 140–41

  Wild Boar Ragú, 95–96

tommygun, 110

Tortilla, The Scoville, 50–52

tortillas:

  Tropical Fish Tacos, 124–25

  Uncle Kyle's Avocado Tacos, 151

tortillas *(continued)*:

  Vegetable Enchiladas with Homemade
    Tomatillo Salsa, 157–59

Tropical Fish Tacos, 124–25

Tuna, Seared, with Wasabi-Coconut Sauce
  and Roasted-Pepper Rice Pilaf, 119–21

Turla, Adam, 163

Tween, Alex, 185

U

Umphrey's McGee, 234

Uncle Kyle's Avocado Tacos, 151

V

Vague Angels, 194

Vanderslice, John, 216

Varldens Basta Pannkaka, 17–18

veal:

  Pasta Bolognese, 75–76

  Roasted Bone Marrow "Battles Style,"
    21–23

Vegan Chocolate Chip Cookies, 228–29

Vegan Sky Juice, 194–95

Vegetable Enchiladas with Homemade
  Tomatillo Salsa, 157–59

Vegetarian Paella, 138–39

Veggie Sausage and Peanut Butter
  Sandwich, 64

Velvet Teen, 132

Venable, Brian, 152

Violent Femmes, 95

Viva Voce, 55

Voxtrot, 178, 187

W

Walkmen, 112

Walla, Chris, 64

walnuts:

  Chocolate Balls, 199–200

  Chocolate Chip Pie, 226–27

walnuts (*continued*):
    Healthy Green Cookies,
       230–31
Ward, Keri, 69
Ward, M., 69
Wasabi-Coconut Sauce, Seared Tuna
    with Roasted-Pepper Rice Pilaf and,
    119–21
Wedren, Craig, 32
We Vs. the Shark, 46
White, Margaret, 226
Wild Boar Ragú, 95–96
Williams, Ian, 21
Williams, Jamie, 232
Windsor for the Derby, 115
Wolf Fish *a l'Italia,* 122–23
Wraight, Tristan, 40

Y

Yamano, Naoko, 230
Yasuda, Toko, 38
The "You Can Care If You Wanna"
    Sandwich, 71–72
Young, Jean, 216

Z

zucchini:
    Chicken Filo Pesto Parcel with Puy Puy,
      105–7
    Kudzu Kurry, 149
    Spiced Tofu Stir-Fry, 163–64
    Tofu Scramble, 6
    Vegetable Enchiladas with Homemade
      Tomatillo Salsa, 157–59
    Zucchini Slippers, 48–49